The
Date Night
Cookbook

The Date Night Cookbook

NED & ARIEL FULMER

WITH KIANO MOJU

The Countryman Press
A Division of W. W. Norton & Company
Independent Publishers Since 1923

Be careful before trying any new foods, especially if you suffer from any food allergies. Needless to say, the authors' views about the benefits of alcohol are not intended as an endorsement of drinking too much, drinking before driving, or drinking at all for anyone who is or thinks they may be an alcoholic. The fermentation described in one of the recipes involves some risks. If you have never done fermented before, do a little research first to make sure you know what kinds of cautions to take.

For information about permission to reproduce selections from this book, write to Permissions, The Countryman Press, 500 Fifth Avenue, New York, NY 10110

For information about special discounts for bulk purchases, please contact W. W. Norton Special Sales at specialsales@wwnorton.com or 800-233-4830

Manufacturing by Toppan Leefung Pte. Ltd.
Book design by Allison Chi
Production manager: Devon Zahn

Library of Congress Cataloging-in-Publication Data

Names: Fulmer, Ned, author. | Fulmer, Ariel, author. | Moju, Kiano, author.
Title: The date night cookbook / Ned & Ariel Fulmer with Kiano Moju.
Description: First edition. | New York : The Countryman Press, a division of W. W. Norton & Company Independent Publishers Since 1923, [2021] | Includes index.
Identifiers: LCCN 2021013869 | ISBN 9781682686539 | ISBN 9781682686546 (epub)
Subjects: LCSH: Cooking for two. | LCGFT: Cookbooks.
Classification: LCC TX652 .F85 2021 | DDC 641.5/612—dc23
LC record available at https://lccn.loc.gov/2021013869

The Countryman Press
www.countrymanpress.com

A division of W. W. Norton & Company, Inc.
500 Fifth Avenue, New York, NY 10110
www.wwnorton.com

10 9 8 7 6 5 4 3 2 1

For our kids,
may you always find love in the kitchen.

Contents

Introduction

Dating is tough! In today's fast-paced world of Tinder and take-out, what we're about to tell you may sound outrageous, but it's true: there's no better way to get to know a person you're dating than through a home-cooked meal. Seriously, whether you're serving up a sensational sage and butter roast chicken or a cozy spaghetti and meatball marinara in your pajamas, food can be the cornerstone of any relationship. Take it from us: while you may not remember what you had for breakfast today, you will always remember what you ate on your first date with your partner— those memories stick with you. That's certainly been our experience, which is exactly why we compiled a cookbook of our favorite stories, advice, and recipes from our over 10 years of dating.

We're Ned and Ariel Fulmer, stars of the YouTube show *Date Night* and members of the Try Guys family. Food is a big part of our relationship—and our online personalities—and as our relationship has grown, so has our appreciation for a good home-cooked meal. Online, we love exploring the differences between home cooking versus the restaurant experience, and we've always dreamed of writing a cookbook filled with beautiful photos. What follows is part storytelling, part cooking advice, part dating advice, and 100 percent woven throughout with love from our kitchen.

Relationships are about putting in the effort and trying new things, and guess what? So is cooking. Mind blown, right? Cooking and relationships go hand in hand. It's all about experimentation and learning. We love the process of exploring new flavors together—like the time we went overboard acquiring a pantry of curry paste and rice noodles at the Thai market, or discovering new techniques—like when we bought a pasta roller on a whim and ate soggy pappardelle for a week. We've been using the same cast-iron pan that we got for our wedding over 10 years ago, and, like a strong relationship, there is a peace in being able to return to something so dependable and perfectly seasoned.

Cooking together doesn't mean you have to love all the same foods. Don't think your soul mate is sitting across the bar just because they ordered the same ravioli. On the contrary, Ned loves steak and Ariel hasn't eaten red meat since she was 17, but food can be a great equalizer. Having disparate tastes can inspire creativity and introduce you to worlds of flavor that you never knew existed. Food is a way to learn about each other, and making meals together is a great way to show affection and unwind at home. We look forward to spending time cooking together every day because, in the end, food is about being together.

And that's what this book is about: connection through cooking.

Whether you're single AF or so married you have a standing Wednesday date night, these recipes are for you. From first dates to moving in and meeting the parents, we want these recipes to take you through every stage of a relationship, with all its ups and downs. Our hope is that you find inspiration in these pages to put down the Postmates, dust off your oven, and open up your heart and kitchen to find love through cooking.

Notes on Organization and Equipment

Organization

The recipes in this book are laid out by the stages of a relationship, starting with first dates and getting to know each other, then moving on to dating exclusively, fighting, meeting family and friends, and finally, commitment. The order of the recipes is based on our own experience and cooking journey, but every relationship is unique and won't follow the same path as ours. Feel free to mix it up and cook with your heart. They're all delicious, so skip ahead and get married after the first date if you want!

We have tailored the recipes so that most of the ingredients and techniques are extremely accessible and inexpensive. Most items should be readily available at a local grocery store or farmers' market, but there are a couple obscure items, such as certain spice blends or sauces, that may be easier to get online or at a specialty store. For those items, we have tried to use them in multiple recipes to cut down on the number of specialty items to buy. There is also an appendix with recipes of easy homemade options for frequently store-bought items and sauces if you'd prefer to do it yourself.

When possible, we recommend fresh vegetables, fruits, and meat over preserved, but, hey, life comes at you fast, and we love pantry staples like dried pasta, rice, and canned food. As much as possible, we have tried to include a variety of dietary options and alcohol-free alternatives, but you may notice that we love pasta and cheese. Especially pasta. OMG, we love pasta. In the current world of low-carb, gluten- and lactose-free options, we realize that may be a bit abnormal, so if you're sensitive, feel free to substitute with an alternative of your choice. And enjoy!

Equipment

First things first: stock your kitchen with some cooking essentials. For kitchen items, it's all about quality over quantity, and these are the very basic kitchen items that we think you'll need to cook date night–worthy dishes at home (and probably more than we had when we started dating). If you already have a stocked kitchen, you can skip this part, but for those just starting out, read on for the necessities.

KNIVES AND CUTTING BOARDS

We recommend having at least two good knives on hand: a chef's knife and a paring knife (or "big knife" and "small knife," as we like to call them). A sturdy cutting board is a necessity as well for chopping veggies and meats. They come in all sizes and materials, but a heavy wooden one is great because it can double as a serving platter.

UTENSILS AND MEASURING

A solid set of kitchen utensils will last you a long time. Our set includes a can opener, vegetable peeler, whisk, metal tongs, stirring spoon, slotted spoon, and spatula. Our personal favorites are silicone spatulas and spoons because they hold up great under heat and won't scratch nonstick pans. It's also good to have a set of measuring cups and spoons for baking as well as a liquid measuring cup. (Yes, there is a difference between dry and liquid measurements!)

POTS AND PANS

A medium or 9-inch skillet with a lid and a medium saucepan with a lid are the go-tos in our kitchen. We like stainless steel because they last forever, but non-stick pots and pans are amazingly easy to use and work for pretty much everything. If you can swing it, we also recommend a sturdy, shallow cast-iron frying pan and an enamel dutch oven for meat, soups, and bread because they keep an even temperature for a longer period of time and can go back and forth from stovetop to oven. Lastly, you'll need at least one sheet pan and shallow baking dish for veggies and desserts.

FOOD PREP AND STORAGE

Two large mixing bowls and two large prep bowls should be all you need for a highly functional kitchen. Ours are ceramic with a nonskid bottom, which is incredibly helpful when using a hand mixer. Glass or metal prep bowls are great as well—you can get them with lids so they double as storage containers. We love glass containers with plastic lids for leftovers because you can see what needs to be eaten. You'll also need a colander or strainer for pasta, rice, and boiled veggies.

EATING AND SERVING

Four sets of plates, bowls, and mugs are usually enough when you're only cooking for one or two people, but if you like to entertain, scale up to sets of eight. The same goes for cutlery, which is usually knives, spoons, and forks but could also include things you use regularly, such as chopsticks, salad forks, and soup spoons. For drinks, highball and lowball glasses are standard for most cocktails, and both are great for everyday things such as juice or water. Wine doesn't necessarily have to go in wine glasses, but if that's your choice, always get more wine glasses than you think you'll need because, if you're like Ned, you'll break about three per year.

CHAPTER 1

Attraction

You never know when you're going to meet the love of your life. We met at a friend's birthday party, and the rest is history. Take it from every romantic comedy ever: you'll be walking down the street with your eyes on your phone and run into the only other cute singleton on the street. Or they'll open a car door right onto your bike. Or they'll walk into your local bookstore, looking for a quirky-yet-delicious cookbook. Anyway, as adorable as they are, meet-cutes hardly ever happen that way, but love does pop up in unexpected places. Prep yourself to make a few simple but impressive meals for two and you'll always be ready for a little romance.

~~~~~~~~~~

Corn and Chicken Tacos

Spicy Jalapeño Icebreaker Margarita

Vegetarian Cavatappi Salad with Pea Tendrils

Blind Date Teriyaki Salmon

Flaky Fruit Tart

Ned's Spaghetti & Meatballs

Love at First Steak with Balsamic Reduction

Last-Minute Cacio e Pepe Bucatini

Maple Blackberry Mojito

Third Date Pizza

Night-In Chocolate Bark

Morning After Avocado Toast

Perfect Eggs Four Ways

~~~~~~~~~~

Corn and Chicken Tacos

SERVES 2

Our first time cooking for one another took place in Ned's basement apartment in Wrigleyville, Chicago. It was a tiny space in the heart of a major sports district that he shared with a roommate. The rent was good, but the kitchen was not. In the rear of the unit, illuminated by fluorescent lights and a thin slit of window, it was dark and barren. The heat didn't work particularly well, so for our first home-cooked meal together, we were still wearing our coats. Ned was cooking a "meal to impress," but since he only knew how to cook one or two things, it was not, uh, particularly impressive. The recipe was, roughly, put chopped chicken breast in a pan, add canned corn, add salsa . . . serve on cold flour tortilla? Despite the food's simplicity and the no-frills space, when you're young and in love, even just the gesture of making food for your partner can be romantic. All you truly need is each other. And letting your new flame into your personal space is a vulnerable first step that can make your bond even deeper. We still fondly remember that night, with all its lack of decor or creature comforts, as one of the most romantic nights of our budding relationship.

INGREDIENTS

Chicken, chopped
Corn
Salsa
Tortillas

INSTRUCTIONS

1. Cook chicken.
2. Add corn and salsa.
3. Serve on cold tortilla.

JUST KIDDING—here are a few tips to make this recipe a little better.

INGREDIENTS

2 (7- to 8-ounce) boneless
    chicken breasts
Salt and pepper
Olive oil
2 cloves garlic, chopped
½ yellow onion, diced
1 can corn, whole kernels
1 can chunky medium salsa
1 teaspoon unsalted butter
4 flour tortillas

INSTRUCTIONS

1. Slice chicken into ¼-inch strips, cut each strip into 2 to 3 pieces, season on all sides with salt and pepper.

2. Heat a saucepan over medium heat and add olive oil to coat the bottom. Add garlic and onion and cook until fragrant, about 1 minute.

3. Add chopped chicken and sear until browned, about 2 minutes on each side.

4. Add corn and salsa, stirring until the entire mixture is heated, about 2 minutes. Remove from heat.

5. Add butter to a frying pan set to medium heat and melt until it sizzles.

6. Toast tortillas on each side until they brown, about 1 minute.

7. Serve chicken mixture on warm tortillas.

Spicy Jalapeño Icebreaker Margarita

SERVES 2

Ned swears he brought a bottle of classy red wine to the party where we first met. I distinctly remember it being tequila, which wasn't an issue since we both love mixing tequila cocktails. This is our go-to "icebreaker" cocktail with a little kick! Everyone's spice levels are different, so we recommend serving these pretty mild to start a conversation about food or travel.   —Ariel

INGREDIENTS

- 2 to 6 fresh jalapeño slices (remove seeds for less spice), plus more for garnish
- 1 ounce agave syrup
- 1½ ounces lime juice
- ½ ounce triple sec or orange liqueur
- 3 ounces tequila
- Lime wedges
- Kosher salt (optional)

INSTRUCTIONS

1. In a mixing glass, muddle jalapeño slices with a muddler or a spoon.
2. Add in agave, lime juice, triple sec, and tequila.
3. Add ice and cover glass.
4. Hold both ends firmly and shake vigorously for 5 to 10 seconds.
5. If desired, run a lime wedge around the rims of two empty glasses and salt the rims.
6. Pour mixture evenly into the two glasses.
7. Garnish with a lime wedge and jalapeño.

Sparkling Jalapeño Limeade (Nonalcoholic)

SERVES 2

INGREDIENTS

2 to 6 fresh jalapeño slices
(remove seeds for less spice),
plus more for garnish

2 ounces agave syrup

2 ounces lime juice

Kosher salt (optional)

Lime wedges

12 ounces seltzer

~~~~~~~~

TIP: For any shaken cocktails,
use a mason jar with a lid.

INSTRUCTIONS

1. In a large mixing glass, muddle jalapeño slices with a muddle or a spoon.

2. Add in agave and lime juice.

3. Add ice and cover glass.

4. Hold both ends firmly and shake vigorously for 5 to 10 seconds.

5. If desired, run a lime wedge around the rims of two tall glasses and salt the rims.

6. Pour mixture evenly into the two glasses.

7. Add 6 ounces of seltzer to each glass.

8. Garnish with lime wedges and jalapeño.

Meeting Cute

Ned: Ariel and I met in Chicago a long time ago, in the prehistoric world before dating apps. Well, not that long ago, but we did meet over 10 years ago, and we met *gasp* *IRL*. We met at our mutual friend Becca's birthday party back in 2009. Becca was a close college friend of mine, and Ariel was one of her new coworkers. Becca often complained to me that she didn't have many female friends since she was new to Chicago. So, upon entering Becca's birthday party, I was expecting it to be all guys.

Ariel: Becca and I were two of the very few young people who worked at a private art conservation company in Chicago. We had a group lunch table for the office and one day, after sitting quietly together making small talk for weeks, I said, "We should be friends!" She laughed and then promptly agreed and invited me to her birthday party with the warning that she "didn't have many girlfriends," and that "most of [her] friends were guys." As a single 24-year-old, I said,

"That's not a problem for me." I told her I'd bring a friend to even things out a little.

Ned: I walked into Becca's birthday party and saw this gorgeous angel across the room from me. She was laughing and smiling, and her eyes sparkled with wit and charm. I had to get to know her better. But the only open seat was on the opposite side of the room from her! I took it and started chatting with her friend to try to seem like I was cool and sociable. I remember bringing a bottle of red wine.

Ariel: OK, it was definitely a half-drunk bottle of tequila instead of red wine.

Ned: Uh, I'm *pretty sure* it was wine—

Ariel: Definitely tequila. Ned immediately started hitting on my friend, Annelise. They had a lot in common—they were both in classes at Improv Olympic and had some of the same teachers—so I comforted myself with the fact that at least she was having a good time.

Ned: It was really more like polite small talk, thank you very much. Really, I kept trying to find ways to talk to Ariel. Slowly over the course of the night, I worked my way around the room—stealing other people's seats whenever they went to the bathroom or got up to get a drink—until I was sitting right next to her. We talked for the rest of the evening as if we were the only two people in the room.

Ariel: I was smitten.

Ned: Me too. As Ariel left the party, I forgot to ask for her phone number and was so sad because I thought I would never see her again.

Ariel: On the walk to the train on the way home, Annelise and I chatted about "that guy Ned." She wasn't particularly interested in dating another guy from the improv world. Excellent. I staked my claim.

Ned: Fortunately, Becca could take a hint and invited us both to a few group trivia nights. Whenever we sat together, the rest of the world felt like it melted away.

Tips for First and Second Dates

When you're cooking at home for a first or second date, here are a few things we like to keep in mind:

- **VET YOUR DATE.** Don't invite someone into your home unless you or someone you know has met them before. And use your instincts! It's always OK to cut a date short if it starts to feel weird.
- **SET THE TABLE.** Creating ambiance by having a space set for your date makes it feel special

- **PREPARE, PREPARE, PREPARE.** Do as much as you can before your date arrives so that when they do get there, all your focus can be on them.
- **HAVE DRINKS AND APPS READY.** Plan for a few moments of chitchat before you sit down. Having drinks and small edibles already prepared makes the transition to a seated meal more seamless.

- **PLAN AN OUT.** You may end up talking late into the night, but if the date isn't going as hoped, plan a friendly reason for them to leave, like having a roommate come home or a friend call for an important chat.

Springtime in Chicago

Homemade pasta for a *Lady and the Tramp* moment

A date at Medieval Times

Vegetarian Cavatappi Salad with Pea Tendrils

SERVES 2, WITH LEFTOVERS

Don't be caught off guard if your date doesn't eat meat (like Ned and his giant meatball fiasco, see page 30)! We are always trying to come up with meatless alternatives in our household since Ariel doesn't eat red meat. Pasta is always a safe choice, and adding a homemade pesto and greens to basic pantry and freezer items makes this meal as delicious as it is beautiful.

INGREDIENTS

8 ounces cavatappi, spiral pasta, or fusilli

¾ cup pesto (store-bought or homemade, see page 214)

1 cup frozen peas, thawed

2 cups pea tendrils or arugula

Juice of 1 lemon

Salt and pepper, to taste

4 ounces feta, crumbled

INSTRUCTIONS

1. Bring a pot of lightly salted water to a boil and cook pasta according to package directions. Drain and allow to cool.

2. If making the pesto from scratch, follow the recipe on page 214. Set aside.

3. In a large mixing bowl, combine pasta, pesto, peas, pea tendrils, and lemon juice. Adjust salt and pepper if desired.

4. Sprinkle feta on top before serving.

Blind Date Teriyaki Salmon

SERVES 2

The oven is your best friend when cooking for someone you just met. It sure was for us. On one of our first dates at home, we sprung for some salmon fillets that we glazed with a sweet teriyaki sauce. What we forgot was that once you put the fillets in the oven, they only take about 10 to 15 minutes to cook. We ended up getting so absorbed in our conversation that we forgot to take them out altogether! Crispy is fine, but if the fire alarm goes off, you may find yourself having an awkward meal.

INGREDIENTS

SALMON

½ cup teriyaki sauce (store-bought or homemade, see page 214)

1-inch piece ginger, peeled and sliced

2 cloves garlic, crushed

2 (6-ounce) salmon fillets

1 green onion, finely sliced

1 teaspoon toasted sesame seeds

KALE

1 tablespoon olive oil

1 clove garlic, sliced

½-inch piece ginger, peeled and sliced

3 cups roughly chopped kale

Salt and pepper, to taste

INSTRUCTIONS

1. In a quart bag or small baking dish, combine teriyaki sauce, ginger, and garlic. Place salmon inside, coating to marinate. If using a baking dish, place the garlic and ginger underneath the salmon with the skin facing up, then cover with teriyaki sauce. Marinate the salmon in the refrigerator for at least 1 hour.

2. Preheat the oven to 400°F. Remove the salmon from the marinade, reserving the leftover sauce for glaze, and place salmon skin down on a parchment-lined baking sheet.

3. Bake for 10 to 15 minutes or until the salmon begins to flake, then move the pan to the top rack to broil until the top of the salmon starts to color, about 1 to 3 minutes—watch closely.

4. To prepare the glaze, simmer reserved marinade in a saucepan over medium heat until thickened, about 10 minutes.

5. To prepare the kale, set a frying pan over medium heat. Add the oil, garlic, and ginger and cook until fragrant, 1 to 2 minutes.

6. Add the kale, season with salt and pepper, then cover with a lid and cook for 3 to 5 minutes until the kale is wilted but still a vibrant green.

7. Serve salmon with the skin down and the kale on the side. Brush the top of the fish with the glaze and garnish with green onion slices and sesame seeds.

Flaky Fruit Tart

SERVES 2, WITH LEFTOVERS

Want to know one of our favorite date night activities? Get your mind out of the gutter! It's eating dessert! Dessert is such a special way to cap off a meal in a way that you wouldn't normally when eating alone. This flaky fruit tart is so easy and delicious. Pop it in the oven about 30 minutes before your date is scheduled to arrive and they'll be greeted with the smell of delicious baked goods.

INGREDIENTS

1 sheet frozen puff pastry, thawed

2 cups (about 2 large peaches) sliced fresh peaches

3 tablespoons light brown sugar

¼ teaspoon cinnamon

Pinch of salt

Milk, for brushing on pastry

Whipped cream (store-bought or homemade, see page 216)

INSTRUCTIONS

1. Preheat the oven to 400°F.

2. Cut pastry into a large circle, about 9 inches in diameter, and place on a parchment-lined baking sheet.

3. In a bowl, toss together the peaches, sugar, cinnamon, and salt. Leaving about an inch around the edge, arrange the peaches in concentric circles on top of the puff pastry, slightly overlapping each slice.

4. Pull the edges of the pastry over the peaches to create a decorative crust and brush the pastry edges with milk.

5. Bake for 20 minutes until golden brown. Cool on a rack.

6. Prepare whipped cream and serve on cooled tart.

First Fancy Date

After meeting up in groups and going out a few times casually, I finally managed to schedule my first fancy date with Ariel. It was at an Italian restaurant in Lakeview, Chicago, near where we both lived, complete with a reservation and everything! We got dressed up, wore our nicest scarves and gloves, and entered the warm and cozy restaurant, full of exposed brick and bustling servers.

On the menu, I was immediately drawn to their signature item, spaghetti with a *1-pound meatball*. I ordered it. Splitting a big meatball sounded like a pretty fun dinner date activity. But it was GIANT. It was bigger than my head. The size of a cantaloupe. It was a truly impractical yet extravagant dish.

When I suggested that we start divvying up this monstrosity, Ariel had a surprised look on her face. "I thought you ordered that for yourself," she said.

I was confused. "I thought we were going to split it."

It was at this point that I learned that Ariel does not eat red meat or pork.

I had made a crucial error in ordering. I was now staring down, solo, at the prospect of a pound of meat that looked more and more like a delicious Italian cannonball about to sink my stomach.

Furthermore, with our relationship still so young and fragile, I felt like I now had something to prove—like eating the entire thing would be some Herculean feat of love. So I began chipping away at this giant meat sphere, and we had a lovely dinner. By the end, I was very full but I realized that if this person was as special to me as I thought she was, she'd understand having a doggy bag.

I had leftovers for days. Ever since then, we've loved making spaghetti and meatballs together and laughing at my machismo.

—Ned

We look so young!

Ned and the 1-pound meatball

Ned's Spaghetti & Meatballs

SERVES 2, WITH LEFTOVERS

Treat your date to a meal worthy of *Lady and the Tramp* by serving meatballs on a big, satisfying plate of spaghetti with a glass of red wine (or Ariel's personal favorite to drink with any meal—a cold glass of Chardonnay). You can make the meatballs whatever size you want, but we've found palm-sized, or about 2 ounces, is best for leftovers. We've included both meat and vegetarian recipes for this Italian staple that are equally delicious. Pro tip: Make the meatball mixture the day before and store in the fridge for the best flavor.

INGREDIENTS

BEEF MEATBALLS

1 pound ground beef

¾ cup plain bread crumbs

½ cup whole milk

⅓ cup grated Parmesan

¼ medium yellow onion, finely diced

1 teaspoon dried oregano

1 large egg

Salt and pepper, to taste

VEGGIE MEATBALLS

3 tablespoons olive oil

12 ounces mushrooms, finely chopped

½ medium yellow onion, finely diced

½ cup quick-cooking rolled oats

½ cup plain bread crumbs

⅓ cup grated Parmesan

1 teaspoon dried oregano

2 large eggs

Salt and pepper, to taste

PASTA

½ pound spaghetti

2 tablespoons olive oil

2 garlic cloves, sliced

½ teaspoon red chili flakes

1 (28-ounce) can crushed tomatoes

Salt and pepper, to taste

½ cup fresh basil leaves

Grated Parmesan, to serve

INSTRUCTIONS

TO MAKE THE BEEF MEATBALLS

1. Preheat the oven to 350°F.

2. In a large mixing bowl, combine all the meatball ingredients. Use your hands to mix together until well combined.

3. Divide and shape into 8 balls, about 2 ounces each, and set rolled meatballs onto a parchment-lined baking sheet. Bake for 20 to 25 minutes until browned.

CONTINUED

TO MAKE THE VEGGIE MEATBALLS

1. Preheat the oven to 400°F.

2. Heat a large saucepan over medium-high heat. Add 2 tablespoons olive oil, mushrooms, and onion and sauté until the liquid has cooked off and the mushrooms have slightly browned, about 10 minutes.

3. Add cooked mixture to a large mixing bowl. Combine all the remaining veggie meatball ingredients and use your hands to mix until well combined. Season with additional salt and pepper to taste.

4. Allow to chill in the fridge for at least 2 hours, up to overnight.

5. Divide and shape into 8 to 10 balls. Set the shaped meatballs onto a parchment-lined baking sheet. Drizzle the tops with 1 tablespoon oil, gently rolling the balls to coat completely. Bake 12 to 15 minutes until the bottoms have browned and they're firm in texture.

TO MAKE THE PASTA

1. Bring a pot of lightly salted water to a boil and cook pasta according to package directions. Drain and allow to cool.

2. Add olive oil, garlic, and chili flakes to a saucepan and set over medium-low heat. Once garlic is fragrant, add the tomatoes and season with salt and pepper. Bring to a gentle simmer and add the cooked meatballs. Simmer for an additional 5 minutes.

3. Turn off heat and stir sauce into the cooked and drained pasta, tossing to coat. Serve with fresh basil and grated Parmesan.

Questions for a First Date

Nervous about a first date? Worried you won't make an impression? People like to talk about themselves, so prep yourself with some good introductory questions and relax! These are some of our go-to conversation options to help gauge if you have a connection and get to know your areas of compatibility more quickly.

What did you do this weekend?

Is there anything you don't eat? Any foods you absolutely love?

What is the thing you love most about yourself?

What do you never get tired of doing? Is there a chore that you would pay $100 for someone to do for you?

What do you do all day? What does a typical day look like for you?

(Better than "What do you do?" since more and more people have nontraditional jobs)

Do you have any pet peeves about other people?

Seen any good movies or TV shows? Anything you could watch over and over again on repeat?

Any fun vacations planned? What would your perfect vacation look like?

What are your close friends like? How did you meet your best friend?

Where is "home"? Are you close with your family?

What's the best job you've ever had? The worst?

Love at First Steak with Balsamic Reduction

SERVES 2

The care that goes into a perfectly cooked sirloin can make even a simple meal feel special, which is what makes steak the ultimate date night food. One of our most memorable dates was at Rosebud Steakhouse in Chicago early in our relationship. We were putting on the ritz, spending our entire monthly dining budget on one meal at this old-money, rich-mahogany, leather-booth steakhouse. But the steak? Perfection. Ned is particularly fond of this recipe, where the balsamic reduction adds a kick of acidity to the rich and savory sirloin and we like to use fresh rosemary from our garden.

INGREDIENTS

2 (8-ounce) sirloin steaks, around 1 inch thick
Kosher salt
Freshly ground black pepper
Sunflower or other neutral oil
1 sprig fresh rosemary
2 large garlic cloves, chopped
½ cup balsamic vinegar

INSTRUCTIONS

1. Season both sides of the steak with salt and a generous amount of pepper, and allow the steaks to come to room temperature before cooking.

2. Heat a frying pan over medium-high heat. Add enough oil to coat the bottom of the pan, and add fresh rosemary and garlic to season the oil. Add in the steaks when the pan is hot, keeping a bit of space between them. The steak should sizzle immediately when it hits the pan. Then lower the heat to medium.

3. Once the bottom of the steaks has formed a thick crust, 3 to 4 minutes, use tongs to flip and cook the steaks on the other side. Once the other side has formed a crust, use tongs to sear the sides. Cook the steaks to desired doneness. If your steak is browned but still needs to cook further, you can finish cooking in a preheated oven set to 400°F.

4. Allow the steak to rest on a cutting board for 10 minutes before serving or slicing. This allows the juices to settle and keeps the steaks moist inside. While the steaks are resting, prepare the balsamic reduction.

5. Add the balsamic vinegar to a small saucepan set over medium heat. Bring to a simmer and reduce until the mixture thickly coats the back of a spoon. This will take 3 to 5 minutes, depending on the width of your pan. Serve alongside or drizzle on top of the steaks.

Last-Minute Cacio e Pepe Bucatini

SERVES 2

Impromptu dates are often the most magical. If you're running behind or are too stressed to make anything challenging, try Cacio e Pepe, an italian dish that translates to "cheese and pepper." It's surprisingly easy and takes just three ingredients. Light a candle, put on fancy pants, take a deep breath, and all of a sudden you're a romantic. Buona sera!

INGREDIENTS

- ½ **pound bucatini or thick spaghetti**
- 1½ **teaspoons freshly ground coarse black pepper, plus additional to serve**
- 1 **cup grated Pecorino Romano cheese, plus additional to serve**

~~~~~~~~

TIP: Don't heavily salt your pasta water because Pecorino can be a very salty cheese.

INSTRUCTIONS

1. Bring a pot of lightly salted water to a boil and cook the pasta according to package directions. Reserve about 1 cup of the cooking water, then strain the pasta.

2. Toast the pepper in a dry sauté pan set over medium-high heat until fragrant, 2 to 3 minutes. Lower the heat to medium and add in ½ cup of the reserved pasta water.

3. Add in the cooked pasta, using tongs to stir.

4. Remove the pan from the heat.

5. Sprinkle the Pecorino cheese on the pasta and use tongs to stir, adding small splashes of hot pasta water as needed until the sauce is creamy in texture.

6. Serve with more cheese and a sprinkle of pepper.

Maple Blackberry Mojito

SERVES 2

Very few people know that Ned LOVES sweet pink drinks, like, more than Ariel. If you imagine an outdoor café by the beach, you can bet Ariel will order a glass of white wine and Ned will order one of these sweet and minty mojitos with no regrets. No machismo needed. It just goes to show that you can't judge a book by its cover and you shouldn't judge your date based on their drink choice either. After all, delicious is delicious, despite the color of the cocktail.

INGREDIENTS

4 to 6 blackberries

8 to 12 mint leaves, plus more to serve

1 ounce maple syrup

1½ ounces lime juice

3 ounces white rum

8 ounces seltzer

Lime slices, to serve

INSTRUCTIONS

1. In a large mixing glass, lightly muddle the blackberries and mint.
2. Add in maple syrup, lime juice, and rum.
3. Add ice and cover glass.
4. Hold both ends firmly and shake vigorously for 5 to 10 seconds.
5. Pour mixture evenly into two glasses.
6. Add 4 ounces of seltzer to each glass.
7. Garnish with a lime slice and mint leaf.

Maple Blackberry Seltzer (Nonalcoholic)

SERVES 2

INGREDIENTS

4 to 6 blackberries

8 to 12 mint leaves, plus more to serve

2 ounces maple syrup

2 ounces lime juice

12 ounces seltzer

Lime slices, to serve

INSTRUCTIONS

1. In a large mixing glass, lightly muddle blackberries and mint.
2. Add in maple syrup and lime juice.
3. Add ice and cover glass.
4. Hold both ends firmly and shake vigorously for 5 to 10 seconds.
5. Pour mixture evenly into two glasses.
6. Add 6 ounces seltzer to each glass.
7. Garnish with a lime slice and mint leaf.

Ideas for How to Meet People

The dating landscape changes all the time. The pandemic has made casual dating an uncertain and often dangerous endeavor, but a year ago it seemed like you couldn't go to a bar without checking Tinder or Bumble first. Don't get us wrong, dating apps are a great way to meet people, but if you're tired of swiping or risking your health and are looking for other ways to find your soulmate, try getting back to basics with some of these ideas:

Take a class. We love cooking classes, but you could also try yoga, pottery, boxing, ballroom dancing . . . the list is endless.

Volunteer. Find an organization in your area that you care about and get involved! You'd be surprised how many great young singles sacrifice their nights and weekends for causes ranging from housing and food to animals and the environment.

Join an athletic club. It may seem cliché, but if you care about fitness, the gym is a really good place to look for a date. Go beyond the treadmills, though, and try showing up early for a group class to chat with the other students.

Throw an intimate party. Tell your friends to invite someone you don't know and make an effort to meet everyone. Worked for us!

Try a coworking space. If you're lucky enough to do some of your work remotely, many coworking spaces offer day passes. Just make sure to spend some time in the common areas, like the coffee bar or the café to introduce yourself to other people.

Our dining room table set for a party

Making friends at a football game

Second and third wheeling

Be a third wheel.
If you don't feel comfortable going alone to a bar or a concert, invite a friend who's in a relationship. Take it from us: couples are often the best wingmen.

Ned at a cooking class

Go back to school.
Colleges offer extension programs for all sorts of things. Try a certificate program or a night class on something you've always wanted to learn, and you may just get a promotion while you're at it.

Be open to blind dates.
You may feel like you've been transported back to the 1950s, but sometimes your friends and family are the best judges of character.

Take your eyes off your phone.
Having lunch in a park? Working on your laptop in a coffee shop? Waiting in line at the grocery store? We are all guilty of taking these solitary moments to check our phones, but it's exhilarating to actually look around and open yourself up to a conversation with a stranger.

Third Date Pizza

SERVES 2

Once you're past the formalities of the first few dates and are looking to have some fun, it's time to start cooking together! Meals without a strict recipe, which are easy to customize, such as these fun pizzas, will make your date feel included. Funky add-ins can be great conversation starters (anchovies, anyone?), and the best part is, at the end of the night you get to eat what you made!

INGREDIENTS

16 ounces pizza dough (store-bought or homemade, see page 214)
Olive oil

TOPPING SUGGESTIONS

COOK WITH PIZZA
Cheese
Mozzarella
Goat cheese
Brie

Meat
Cooked sausage, crumbled
Rotisserie chicken, shredded
Pepperoni slices

Veggies
Roasted broccoli
Sun-dried tomatoes
Sautéed mushrooms
Olives, sliced
Onions, caramelized
Pine nuts
Spicy chilies

AFTER COOKING
Meat
Prosciutto slices

Veggies
Arugula
Basil leaves
Rosemary

Sauces
Pesto
Fig jam
Honey

POTENTIAL COMBINATIONS
Chicken, roasted broccoli, pesto, goat cheese

Mushrooms, rosemary, basil, sun-dried tomatoes

Caramelized onion, pine nuts, spicy sausage, sliced olives, pesto

Brie, fig jam, prosciutto, arugula

Mozzarella, pepperoni, spicy chilies, honey

INSTRUCTIONS

1. Preheat the oven to 500°F.

2. Roll pizza dough on a lightly floured surface about the same size as a baking sheet.

3. Use 1 tablespoon of olive oil to grease the baking sheet and lay the pizza dough on top. Lightly brush the dough with olive oil.

4. Top pizza with your bake toppings. Bake for 10 to 15 minutes until the crust is golden and the bottom of the pizza is firm.

5. Remove your pizza from the oven and add any post-bake toppings.

Night-In Chocolate Bark

SERVES 2, WITH LEFTOVERS

Ever tried chocolate on popcorn? Or marshmallows in cereal? You can make all the funky combinations you want with this fun chocolate bark snack. Once you start getting comfortable with your date, plan on a few intimate evenings at home without an agenda apart from a sweet snack and a Netflix queue. Ariel loves a good fruit and nut bark, while Ned likes his a little more junk food–inspired with pretzels and salt. Try one of our combinations and prepare to get cozy.

INGREDIENTS

BARK BASE

½ pound semisweet or dark chocolate

TRAIL MIX (1 CUP TOTAL)

Almonds

Cashews

Pumpkin seeds

Dried cherries, chopped

Dried apricots, chopped

BREAKFAST INSPIRED
(1 CUP TOTAL)

Cornflakes

Mini marshmallows

Dried strawberries

SNACK FOOD INSPIRED
(1 CUP TOTAL)

Small pretzels, broken

Caramel

Flaky sea salt

INSTRUCTIONS

1. Line a baking sheet with parchment or wax paper.

2. To melt the chocolate, place into a microwave-safe bowl. Microwave the chocolate on medium power in 30-second intervals, stirring between each interval until the chocolate is melted and runny.

3. Pour the melted chocolate onto the lined baking sheet. Use a spatula or the back of a spoon to spread the chocolate into a rectangle shape that is ⅛ inch thick.

4. Sprinkle your chosen toppings, gently pressing them into the chocolate.

5. Allow the chocolate to cool in the fridge for 30 minutes or until set. Don't leave it in the refrigerator for too long or the chocolate will develop a whitish film.

6. Once your chocolate has set, peel away the parchment and place on a cutting board. Use a large knife to cut into big chunks.

Advice for Finding Lasting Love from a Couple That's Been Married for, Like, Ever

1. **Make yourself a priority, then look outward for happiness from others.** This is our number one piece of advice. Relationships are not Band-Aids to mitigate your personal issues or boost your self-confidence. You have to value yourself and your needs before you can communicate those needs and contribute to a partnership.

2. **Put in the effort and don't be afraid to look for love.** Ever heard the saying, "You'll find love when you're not looking for it?" It's a myth! Imagine looking for a job by sitting at home, doing nothing. You would be forever unemployed! You have to put yourself out there and make some mistakes in order to figure out what you truly want in a long-term relationship.

3. **Understand your own needs and be up-front about them.** Do you need a lot of space in a relationship? A lot of affection? How do you deal with conflict? Are there deal breakers that you can't tolerate, like cheating or smoking? We learned the hard way that you have to recognize your needs and be honest to give both you and your partner a better chance at a healthier and longer-lasting relationship.

4. **Have realistic expectations.** Many people go into a relationship with expectations based on their past experiences, their family, or the influence of their friends. By all means, you should have standards, but unrealistic expectations can make any future partner seem inadequate. Ned didn't even have a job when he and Ariel met, and now he's famous! Be willing to evaluate weaknesses together and decide if and when you are willing to compromise.

5. **Don't expect that you can change someone.** As much as you may want a relationship to work despite a conflict, it's not fair to expect someone to change for you or the relationship. You are each individual people and you have to love the other person for who they are—anything less can foster resentment and disappointment.

6. **Look for partnership in addition to romance.** Take it from a couple that has been happily married for longer than YouTube has been around: romance can ebb and flow when life gets hectic, but a solid partnership based on respect, trust, communication, support, and fun is what can build you both up as individuals and lead to a happier, more satisfying life.

Morning After Avocado Toast

SERVES 2

While we're not telling THAT story, breakfast has always been an important meal for us, and to this day we still take the time to eat together every morning. Early on, our breakfasts usually consisted of cereal and coffee together. We didn't really know how to make eggs and were often squeezing breakfast in before running off to the train to go to work. After we ate cereal, there would always be a little bit of milk leftover. Ned always liked to drink his, but Ariel found that a little icky. One morning, after Ned drank his own leftover milk, Ariel asked him if he would drink hers, a funny game she used to play with her dad and sister. For her family, the answer would always be a resounding "Ewwww, nooo!" but for Ned it was an "Uhhh, OK!" to which Ariel replied "EWWW, WHAT? I WASN'T SERIOUS!" But it was too late. Ned had already quaffed her leftovers. It's still a story Ariel likes telling to this day because Ned had left such a lasting, if somewhat gross, impression.

INGREDIENTS

2 tablespoons apple cider vinegar

1 teaspoon sugar

2 tablespoons water

Pinch of kosher salt

1 shallot or ¼ red onion, thinly sliced

1 large avocado

1 small lemon, zested and juiced

Flaky sea salt

Two 1-inch-thick slices of crusty bread, toasted

1 tablespoon pumpkin seeds

2 large eggs, cooked any style (see page 54)

INSTRUCTIONS

1. In a small saucepan, bring vinegar, sugar, water, and kosher salt to a simmer. Turn off heat and add the shallot. Stir and allow to sit for at least 10 minutes to allow the onion to absorb the warm vinegar, then drain.

2. In a mixing bowl, place the avocado, lemon juice, and sea salt. Use a fork to mash together.

3. Spread the avocado mash on top of the bread slices. Top with pickled onion, pumpkin seeds, and lemon zest. Serve each with an egg.

Perfect Eggs Four Ways

SERVES 2, EACH

While it's a far cry from our old cereal standby, we recommend you show your date how perfect they are by surprising them with perfect eggs. If you're cooking at your house, it's a delightful gesture. If you're at theirs, though, don't go too crazy. You can use a couple eggs or some milk, but remember you don't live there. And do the dishes when you're done! Any one of these simple egg recipes will show that you care without the big cleanup.

French Omelette

Aaaah, the omelette. Ariel fell in love with omelettes while living in Paris as a teenager (that's also where she fell in love with fries). The American version is usually stuffed with veggies and cheese, but we prefer the French omelette: just butter, eggs, and a sprinkle of herbs. Goes great with a side salad (or fries TBH).

INGREDIENTS

4 large eggs
Salt and pepper
2 tablespoons unsalted butter

INSTRUCTIONS

1. In a bowl, whisk together eggs with salt and pepper.

2. Heat an 8-inch nonstick skillet set over medium-low heat. Add in the butter, swirling to coat the bottom of the pan.

3. Once the butter has melted and is slightly foamy, pour in the eggs. Use a soft spatula to gently move the eggs around for the first few seconds of cooking. Swirl the pan to allow uncooked egg to coat the bottom. Once the bottom is set, fold into thirds and serve.

Soft-Boiled Eggs

Soft-boiled eggs go well on anything, from salads to sandwiches to soup. If you're like Ariel and your favorite part of breakfast is actually buttered toast, try spreading a soft-boiled egg on some crispy bread for a warm and gooey snack.

INGREDIENTS

4 large eggs, room temperature

INSTRUCTIONS

1. Bring a medium-sized pot filled with water to a boil over high heat. Once water is boiling, reduce the heat to medium-high for a more gentle simmer. Use a wooden spoon to gently lower the eggs into the boiling water. Cook for 6 minutes.

2. While eggs are cooking, prepare an ice bath by filling a medium-sized bowl with ice and water. Once eggs are cooked, spoon them out and place in the ice bath to immediately stop the cooking. Peel once cooled.

Froached Eggs

It's not a typo! This is our family classic, inspired by the eggs that Ariel's mom likes to cook. The perfect egg, a little fried and mostly poached. Ariel tried to order them at a diner one time, but it was a massive failure that ended in undercooked, wet eggs. It takes practice and patience, but once mastered you will never look back.

INGREDIENTS

1 tablespoon unsalted butter
4 large eggs
Salt and pepper, to taste

INSTRUCTIONS

1. Heat a medium-sized frying pan over medium-low heat. Melt the butter, then crack the eggs into the pan next to one another.

2. Cook eggs in the butter until the egg whites begin to turn opaque, about 2 minutes.

3. Pour ½ cup water into the side of the pan, then cover. Cook for another 1 to 3 minutes until egg whites are firm and the yolks are cooked to your desired doneness.

4. Use a slotted spatula to remove the eggs, placing them on a paper towel to absorb excess water. Season with salt and pepper. Serve immediately.

Fluffy Scrambled Eggs

Simple and delicious. We have always disagreed on the perfect scrambled eggs. Ned likes his a little runny, while Ariel prefers hers well done. Either way, we've found it's best to beat them well with milk and cook them with butter over low heat and constant love and attention.

INGREDIENTS

4 large eggs, room temperature

2 tablespoons milk

Kosher salt, to taste

2 tablespoons unsalted butter

Freshly ground black pepper, to taste

INSTRUCTIONS

1. Beat eggs and milk together until there are no visible streaks of egg white. Season with a good pinch of salt.

2. Warm a nonstick skillet over medium heat. Add the butter and melt until frothy. Pour in the eggs, then lower the heat to medium-low. Use a soft spatula to gently scramble, moving the spatula in a figure eight, then around the edges. Be sure to scrape the bottom.

3. Once there is about 20 percent of uncooked egg left, remove the pan from the stove. Continue stirring; the residual heat of the pan will cook the rest of the egg. Season with salt and pepper.

CHAPTER 2.

Dating

It's still the infatuation phase, but you guys are officially dating now. Every minute feels like it revolves around you and that special other person. You can't hide from the world together forever, though. Eventually you're going to want to tell your friends you met someone, so don't be afraid to go all out when it comes to those important milestones, like your first double date or throwing your first party as a couple. This chapter includes cozy recipes for two as well as shareable party bites for eight or more.

Cheese Board with Candied Pecans

Ginger Mint Julep

Antipasto Party Skewers

Charred Broccoli Frittata

Smashed Roast Potatoes

Sesame Shrimp Puffs with Sweet Chili Sauce

Italian Shakshuka

All-Season Cookie Party

Fizzy Rosé Paloma

Ginger Garlic Finger Chicken

Chicken and Potato Hand Pies

Crabcake Burgers with Spicy Aioli

Barbecue Blackberry Cobbler

Strawberry Tahini Blondies

Spicy Red Pepper and Feta Dip

Potluck Provençal Pasta Salad

Mozzarella Monkey Bread

Cheese Board with Candied Pecans

SERVES 8

It's no secret that we love cheese. Ariel is the master of the cheese board. Over time, we have become very good at throwing together a good board because it's always a crowd-pleaser. Nothing is wrong with simple cheese and bread, but adding honey, homemade jam or candied pecans, and sliced fruit will take it to the next level. If you're a couple throwing your first dinner party, this is the perfect way to delight your friends.

INGREDIENTS

CANDIED PECANS
½ pound whole pecans
⅔ cup maple syrup
1 teaspoon flaky sea salt

BOARD ELEMENTS
Hard Cheese (choose 1 or 2)
White Cheddar
Pecorino Romano
Parmigiano-Reggiano
Manchego
Aged Gouda

Soft Cheese (choose 1 or 2)
Brie
Goat cheese with honey
Camembert
Blue cheese
Boursin

Fruits
Dried apricots
Pears, sliced
Fig jam (see page 215)

Starch
Water crackers
Baguette, sliced

INSTRUCTIONS

1. To prepare the candied pecans, add the pecans and maple syrup to a nonstick saucepan set over medium heat.

2. Bring to a simmer, tossing to coat the pecans in the syrup.

3. Continue to cook for 3 to 5 minutes, stirring occasionally until there is no visible syrup pooling at the bottom.

4. Pour onto a parchment-lined baking sheet, spreading out so none are overlapping. Sprinkle with sea salt and allow to cool.

~~~~~~

TIP:
To design a stunning cheese board, we suggest:
- Picking a variety of cheeses and textures, we like picking one or two each of hard and soft cheeses.
- Designing with the biggest elements first, like the blocks of cheese and bowls, and finishing with smaller elements like fruits and crackers.

Ginger Mint Julep

SERVES 2

We are both from the South—Texas and Florida—so the julep was a part of the party vocabulary growing up. If you don't want light beer all over your floors, try to infuse a little sophistication into the party with this classic Southern cocktail that appeals to all tastes. This one is great to make in a batch and serve in a pitcher: just multiply the recipe by however many people you plan to serve.

INGREDIENTS

4 slices peeled ginger
8 to 12 fresh mint leaves
1 ounce honey
4 ounces bourbon whiskey
2 fresh mint sprigs, to serve

INSTRUCTIONS

1. In a mixing glass, muddle the ginger and mint.
2. Add the honey and bourbon, then stir to mix thoroughly.
3. Pour mixture evenly into two rocks glasses.
4. Add ice (crushed if available).
5. Garnish with fresh mint sprigs.

Ginger Mint Sweet Tea (Nonalcoholic)

SERVES 2

INGREDIENTS

4 slices peeled ginger
8 to 12 fresh mint leaves
16 ounces iced tea
2 ounces honey
2 fresh mint sprigs, to serve

INSTRUCTIONS

1. In a mixing glass, muddle the ginger and mint.
2. Add iced tea and honey, then stir.
3. Pour mixture evenly into two tall glasses.
4. Add ice (crushed if available).
5. Garnish with fresh mint sprigs.

Antipasto Party Skewers

SERVES 8

At any given party, you can reliably find us next to the snack table. It's how we bonded when we first met. Drinks are great and all, but the real party animals know to go hard for the snacks. These bites have been in our rotation ever since we lived in Chicago because they are so easy to grab and eat. No plate, no fork. One bite and you always have an excuse to leave an awkward conversation to leave and get more food (or talk to the hottie by the snack table!).

Caprese Skewers

INGREDIENTS

1 pint (10 ounces) cherry or grape tomatoes, halved

Kosher salt, to taste

1 tablespoon balsamic vinegar

1 (8-ounce) container ciliegine (small balls) mozzarella

Fresh basil leaves

Olive oil

INSTRUCTIONS

1. In a medium-sized bowl, season tomatoes with salt and balsamic vinegar. Marinate for at least 30 minutes.

2. Using a cocktail-sized toothpick, skewer a mozzarella ball, then tomato half, followed by a basil leaf and another mozzarella ball.

3. Continue to assemble the remaining skewers, arranging onto a serving platter.

4. Lightly drizzle olive oil on top immediately before serving.

Prosciutto and Melon Skewers

INGREDIENTS

½ pound thinly sliced prosciutto

One 1-pound melon, cut into rectangles (1 inch wide, ½ inch thick)

INSTRUCTIONS

1. Cut the prosciutto into long strips.

2. Wrap each piece of melon in a piece of prosciutto, making sure it wraps at least once all the way around.

3. Skewer two wrapped pieces onto a cocktail-sized toothpick.

4. Continue to assemble the remaining skewers, arranging them on a serving platter. Keep refrigerated until ready to serve.

Deli Skewers

INGREDIENTS

30 salami slices (2½ inch thick), each slice cut into 4 triangles

10 provolone cheese slices, each cut into 6 triangles

¼ cup sliced peperoncini

⅓ cup sun-dried tomato, cut into ¼-inch-thick strips

INSTRUCTIONS

1. On a cocktail-sized toothpick, skewer a slice of salami, provolone, pepperoncini, and sun-dried tomato, then repeat.

2. Continue to assemble the remaining skewers, arranging them on a serving platter. Keep refrigerated until ready to serve.

Meeting Friends

While it's nothing compared to meeting the parents, meeting the friends of someone you're dating is a daunting affair. When we first started dating, one of the most suspenseful yet hilarious moments was when Ariel met Ned's college friends.

Ned: I am very close with my college friends. Six of us lived together three out of four years of college, and now we live all across the country but still keep in touch. We actually have been writing a monthly newsletter, giving each other brief updates on our lives, for over 10 years now. We play in the same fantasy football league each year and plan annual reunions to travel and see each other.

Ariel: They're a boisterous bunch. There's no getting a word in edgewise. I was eager to meet the guys that were so important to Ned but had no idea what I was in for. Early on when Ned and I were dating, it was time for Ned's "Boyz" to have a reunion. The selected location was snowy Chicago, crashing on the floor of our new apartment.

Ned: It was like a clown car. One, two, four guys arrived at the apartment back-to-back, each greeted with an even greater chorus of whoops and hugs.

Ariel: I had planned out a cute cocktail hour, but within minutes there were beers being shotgunned in the kitchen. The conversation became more insular—inside jokes about old classmates—and I felt more and more like I was living out a scene from *Animal House*.

Ned: What can I say? This was the first time we had seen each other since college!

Ariel: There was sticky light beer EVERYWHERE. The party went on into the evening, and one guy decided to take a nap on our sofa, which was around the time that everyone thought to warn me that this guy was known to pee on couches in his sleep. But not to worry because it actually only happened twice! I was mortified.

Ned: The weekend eventually was a success because everyone got to know Ariel and Ariel got to see a more nuanced view of my friends.

Ariel: It's certainly an unforgettable first impression, but I did learn that you are fiercely loyal to those you're close with.

Ned: I'm just happy you wanted to continue dating me after that.

Ariel: I'm just happy that [REDACTED] didn't pee on our couch.

Ready for a music festival with Ariel's college friends

Ned on the aforementioned couch

Making Nice with Roommates

In the first few months of our relationship we spent a lot of time at each other's apartments. It was a blissful stage where we lived in our own world and went about our lives as if other people didn't even exist. Every morning we would scarf cereal together before work and grab leftovers from the fridge for lunch. We would then come home from work to get ready to go out or stay in and make a big meal together and watch movies. It was heaven . . . until both our roommates sat us down to explain that the grocery budget was getting a little out of control, there was never any milk left in the fridge, and we had to tone down our midnight movie marathons. As it turns out, other people did exist and they were getting a little fed up.

It's likely that if you're in the early stages of coupledom (and not a multimillionaire), you are living with roommates. Roommates are the best for SO MANY reasons. Aside from cheaper rent, wine nights, and a shoulder to cry on, your roommate could very well be the person that you spend the most time with. When you invite another person into the mix (and into the apartment), things might get challenging, so learn from our mistakes and keep a couple things in mind.

- **COMMON COURTESIES GO A LONG WAY.** If you're at your partner's place, clean up after yourself! Impress them by tidying up or doing the dishes.
- **DON'T LEAVE YOUR THINGS IN SHARED SPACES, EVEN IF YOU ARE BASICALLY LIVING THERE.** If your name isn't on the lease, your toothbrush should not take residence in the shared bathroom.
- **CONTRIBUTE TO GROCERIES.** If you are eating their food regularly, you have an obligation to replace it.
- **LASTLY, MAKE AN EFFORT TO INCLUDE THEM.** Invite them to have brunch, or make a little extra dinner so they can have leftovers for lunch too.

You don't need to go nuts, but we could have saved ourselves a lot of difficult conversations—and honestly some friendships—by making nice early on.

Summer of love

Our first winter together in Chicago

Charred Broccoli Frittata

SERVES 4

Brunch is a seriously underrated date meal. Have your boo over for a quick bite with your roommate before going on a Sunday adventure to the flea market or art museum. This recipe started as Ariel's attempt to make a Spanish "tortilla" and is great for a large group because you can expand it with virtually no extra work. Serve with a simple salad or (our personal favorite) roasted potatoes.

INGREDIENTS

1½ pounds broccoli florets

¼ cup olive oil

Salt and pepper, to taste

6 large eggs

½ cup whole milk

⅔ cup grated Pecorino Romano, plus additional to serve

INSTRUCTIONS

1. Preheat the oven to 450°F. On a parchment-lined baking sheet, toss together broccoli in 3 tablespoons olive oil, seasoning with salt and pepper. Spread onto a flat, even layer and roast until slightly charred, 15 to 20 minutes.

2. Lower the oven temperature to 400°F.

3. In a large mixing bowl, whisk together the eggs, milk, cheese, and more salt and pepper.

4. Add the remaining olive oil to a cast-iron pan, swirling to coat the bottom. Place the roasted broccoli in the pan and pour the egg mixture on top. Bake for 15 minutes or until the egg is set in the center.

5. Sprinkle with additional Pecorino Romano and serve right out of the pan.

Smashed Roast Potatoes

SERVES 4, WITH LEFTOVERS

These are addictive. Seriously, take this as a warning. We love attempting to re-create restaurant meals at home and discovered the "smashing" technique somewhat randomly at a restaurant in Los Angeles. We've never looked back. You get the buttery softness of a boiled potato but with the extra crisp and spice of a roasted potato, all in one tasty bite.

INGREDIENTS

2 pounds baby yellow potatoes
¼ cup olive oil
Salt and pepper, to taste
1 teaspoon granulated garlic
2 tablespoons rosemary leaves

INSTRUCTIONS

1. Preheat the oven the 450°F.

2. Starting from cold, boil the potatoes in a pot of salted water. Cook until fork tender, 8 to 10 minutes, then drain.

3. Place potatoes on a parchment-lined baking sheet. Using the bottom of a clean coffee mug, gently smash the potatoes until slightly flattened.

4. Drizzle with olive oil; season with salt, pepper, granulated garlic, and rosemary; and toss well to coat.

5. Roast until potatoes are crispy, 30 to 35 minutes. Serve immediately.

Sesame Shrimp Puffs with Sweet Chili Sauce

SERVES 8

Sure, you could buy some frozen appetizers at Trader Joe's, but why not make something fresh and different that will make you look like a whiz in the kitchen? One of our oldest party tricks is to try to replicate something you could buy from the freezer aisle. Shrimp paste and puff pastry take just as long to cook as a store-bought alternative, but the flavor is so much better. And puff pastry looks and tastes fancy, but it's actually very easy to use.

INGREDIENTS

1 sheet frozen puff pastry, thawed

1 pound peeled and deveined raw or defrosted shrimp, finely chopped

2 cloves garlic, minced

2 stalks green onion, chopped

1 tablespoon sunflower oil

2 tablespoons soy sauce

1 large egg

1 tablespoon sesame seeds

½ cup sweet chili sauce, to serve

INSTRUCTIONS

1. Preheat the oven to 425°F.

2. Cut the puff pastry into nine squares.

3. Pat the shrimp dry, then add shrimp, garlic, green onion, sunflower oil, soy sauce, and egg to a food processor and pulse into a rough paste. Or chop ingredients and mix in a bowl.

4. Scoop 2 tablespoons of the shrimp mixture onto the center of each pastry square and fold along the center diagonal to create a triangle.

5. Sprinkle the sesame seeds on top.

6. Bake for 15 minutes or until golden brown. Serve with sweet chili sauce on the side.

Italian Shakshuka

SERVES 4

You may be looking at this recipe and thinking, "Tomato sauce for breakfast?" But the answer is a resounding yes, and it's a brunch staple here in Los Angeles. We make ours the Italian way, à la Eggs in Purgatory, with fresh basil to complement the spicy tomatoes. Our recipe packs a little heat, so be sure to have mimosas on hand to cool things down.

INGREDIENTS

¼ cup extra virgin olive oil

4 cloves garlic, sliced

½ large yellow onion, diced

1 teaspoon dried chili flakes

1 (26-ounce) can or container crushed tomatoes

Kosher salt, to taste

1 cup chopped fresh basil

6 large eggs

4 ounces feta cheese

Fresh bread, to serve

INSTRUCTIONS

1. Add olive oil, garlic, onion, and chili flakes to a skillet or braiser and set over medium heat. Once the garlic is fragrant, add the tomatoes, seasoning with salt. Bring to a gentle simmer and add in the basil.

2. Crack the eggs and gently nest them on top of the mixture, evenly spread out, and season with salt on top.

3. Sprinkle on the feta, cover, and let cook for about 5 minutes.

4. Serve right out of the pan with bread for dipping.

Party Ideas

There is an Italian saying that means "good food, good wine, good friends" that we like to live our lives by. There aren't many things better than having friends over for good food. Even in the early stages of our relationship, we would have people over all the time for double dates, TV watch parties, and summer barbecues. It's a great way to combine friend groups and get to know your partner's crew in the most fun way possible. Here are our top 10 party ideas for hosting friends:

1. **Viewing Party:** In those days it was *Friday Night Lights* and *Breaking Bad* for us, but you can pick any show—even reruns—and set out some batch cocktails and appetizers for people to mingle on the sofa.

2. **Double Date:** Invite your bestie (or theirs!) and their beau over for an intimate double date. For an established couple, it's a great way to pick their brain on how they got where they are and tell stories of their early courtship.

3. **Cookie Party:** It's a twist on a holiday tradition, but why save cookies for a special occasion? This one is best for a few friends and an empty Sunday afternoon. We like to make one big batch of cookies and then invite everyone to add in their own mix-ins or bring a family recipe.

4. **Outdoor Barbecue:** Take the cooking outside and turn food prep into a social event! It's instinctive and thrilling to cook food outdoors over a fire, and the central cooking location can bring groups of people together more easily than cooking indoors.

5. **Potluck:** The great thing about a potluck is you can invite 5 or 50 people and the work is about the same. There will be leftovers, though, if everyone brings a dish— that's just math—so plan ahead and have some people bring utensils or drinks.

6. **Brunch:** Why is brunch so fun? Well, it's not as formal as breakfast or lunch, but it can include food from either. Our favorite trick is to set up food stations like loaded waffles, burritos, or bagels instead of a sit-down breakfast to encourage people to mingle. Oh, and bottomless mimosas are never a bad idea.

7. Picnic: There is absolutely nothing wrong with eating cheese as a meal. There, we said it. Bring a blanket and a bottle of wine, and any spread can become a meal with a grassy spot and a good group of friends.

8. Any Special Occasion: Birthdays, engagements, promotions, babies! There are so many obvious reasons to bring people together to celebrate, but we also believe in celebrating some of the less obvious occasions: acing a test, a new haircut, a compliment from a stranger, a particularly strong bowel movement. Heck, invite people over for no reason—just enjoy some food.

9. Game Night: This is Ned's particular favorite. There was a time before we had kids that we played Dungeons & Dragons with other couples for epic eight-hour periods on weekends, interrupted only by meal breaks.

10. Supper Club: We know, the '40s called, but it's fun! Host the same group at a different house every week or every month. Try inviting some new "guests" every time to make things interesting and potentially make some new friends.

Ned with his favorite: a fruity tropical drink!

Dressed up for a birthday party

All-Season Cookie Party

Cookie parties aren't just for the holidays anymore! Ariel loves to make cookies with friends just for the fun of it—and the experience can last for days if everyone goes home with the final product.

Cereal Cookies

MAKES A DOZEN COOKIES

Our version of the childhood everything cookie. We firmly believe that a good, buttery cookie can be a base for anything you want to throw in. So why not Fruity Pebbles? Heck, try Frosted Flakes or crumbled Cinnamon Toast Crunch. There are no wrong answers here.

INGREDIENTS

½ cup light brown sugar, packed

½ cup granulated sugar

1 large egg, room temperature

16 tablespoons (2 sticks) unsalted butter, softened

2 teaspoons vanilla extract

2 cups all-purpose flour

1 teaspoon baking soda

½ teaspoon kosher salt

1½ cups Fruity Pebbles cereal (or your favorite), plus more for topping

INSTRUCTIONS

1. Preheat the oven to 350°F.

2. In a large mixing bowl, whisk together the brown sugar, granulated sugar, egg, butter, and vanilla extract until smooth.

3. Sift the flour, baking soda, and salt into the same bowl and use a rubber spatula to stir until combined.

4. Sprinkle in cereal, folding in gently and being careful not to crush the cereal.

5. Line two baking sheets with parchment paper and scoop ¼-cup portions of cookie dough, leaving 3 inches of space between each cookie. Sprinkle the top of each cookie with a teaspoon of cereal.

6. Bake for 9 to 11 minutes or until the edges have lightly browned. Allow to cool on the baking sheet for 10 minutes before removing from the tray.

Oatmeal Lace Cookies

MAKES 2 DOZEN COOKIES

We make these thin and crispy lace cookies—lighter than a chewy chocolate chip cookie but way more decadent than an oatmeal raisin cookie—with plenty of drizzled chocolate.

INGREDIENTS

- 8 tablespoons (1 stick) unsalted butter
- 1 cup light brown sugar
- 1 cup rolled oats
- 1 tablespoon all-purpose flour
- 1 large egg, room temperature
- ½ cup (3 ounces) chopped dark chocolate
- 1 teaspoon flaky sea salt

INSTRUCTIONS

1. Preheat the oven to 350°F.

2. In a small saucepan set over medium heat, melt together the butter and brown sugar. Do not bring to a simmer. Allow to cool to room temperature.

3. In a mixing bowl, whisk together the oats and flour. Create a well in the center and add the egg and cooled butter-sugar mixture.

4. Starting in the center, whisk together until combined.

5. Line a baking sheet with parchment paper. Use a regular spoon to scoop out the cookies (1 tablespoon each), leaving at least 4 inches between each cookie.

6. Bake for 6 to 8 minutes or until the cookies have spread and are golden brown. Allow cookies to cool on the baking sheet for at least 5 minutes or until cookies have hardened.

7. Melt the chocolate in the microwave on low heat in 20-second intervals until runny, stirring in between.

8. Use a spoon to drizzle the chocolate on top of the cookies, then immediately sprinkle with sea salt while the chocolate is still runny. Allow chocolate to firm, about 30 minutes. Use a spatula to carefully lift cookies off the tray.

Salted Brown Butter Chocolate Chip Cookies

MAKES A DOZEN COOKIES

This is our tried-and-tested recipe for a classic chocolate chip cookie—gooey in the middle and crispy on the sides. Browning the butter before adding it to the mix adds a depth of flavor, and a sprinkle of salt on top enhances and intensifies the flavor.

INGREDIENTS

16 tablespoons (2 sticks) unsalted butter, softened

¾ cup light brown sugar, packed

½ cup granulated sugar

1 large egg, room temperature

2 teaspoons vanilla extract

1⅔ cups all-purpose flour

1 teaspoon baking soda

1 teaspoon kosher salt, plus more for sprinkling

2 cups (12 ounces) semisweet chocolate chips

INSTRUCTIONS

1. Preheat the oven to 350°F.

2. Melt the butter in a medium saucepan over medium heat. Continue to cook, stirring frequently, until the butter turns a light brown color and has a nutty aroma. Allow to cool to room temperature.

3. In a large mixing bowl, whisk together the brown sugar, granulated sugar, egg, browned butter, and vanilla extract until smooth.

4. Sift the flour, baking soda, and salt into the same bowl. Use a rubber spatula to stir until combined.

5. Gently fold in the chocolate chips so they are evenly distributed.

6. Line two baking sheets with parchment paper and scoop on ¼-cup portions of cookie dough, leaving 3 inches of space between each cookie. Sprinkle with salt.

7. Bake for 9 to 11 minutes or until the edges have lightly browned. Allow to cool on the baking sheet for 10 minutes before removing from the tray.

Fizzy Rosé Paloma

SERVES 2

Tired of mimosas at your brunch party? Rosé is already a summer classic, but to mix things up, we add grapefruit and tequila to make the daytime buzz even more delicious. This one makes a great batch cocktail for a larger group because the sweet and tangy mixture is an easy crowd-pleaser—just multiply the recipe by the number of people you want to serve.

INGREDIENTS

2 ounces tequila

2 ounces rosé

1 ounce agave syrup

1½ ounces lime juice

3 ounces grapefruit juice

4 ounces seltzer water

2 slices lime and/or grapefruit, for garnish

INSTRUCTIONS

1. Combine tequila, rosé, agave, lime juice, and grapefruit juice in mixing glass and mix thoroughly.

2. Pour evenly into two rocks glasses with ice.

3. Top with seltzer water.

4. Garnish with a slice of lime and/or grapefruit.

Fizzy Paloma (Nonalcoholic)

SERVES 2

INGREDIENTS

2 ounces agave syrup

2 ounces lime juice

6 ounces grapefruit juice

8 ounces seltzer

2 slices lime and/or grapefruit, for garnish

INSTRUCTIONS

1. Combine agave, lime juice, and grapefruit juice in mixing glass and mix thoroughly.

2. Pour evenly into two tall glasses with ice.

3. Top with seltzer water.

4. Garnish with a slice of lime and/or grapefruit.

Ginger Garlic Finger Chicken

SERVES 8

Ariel's sister, Danielle, showed up to a *Game of Thrones* watch party with these chicken appetizers, and they were so mouth-wateringly delicious we immediately added them to our recipe book. Plan on at least a few pieces per person because it's impossible to eat just one!

INGREDIENTS

1 cup teriyaki sauce (store-bought or homemade, see page 214)

2 pounds chicken tenderloin

2 teaspoons sesame seeds, to serve

Chives, thinly sliced, to serve

INSTRUCTIONS

1. Add teriyaki sauce to a large mixing bowl. Add the chicken, tossing to coat well. Cover with plastic wrap and refrigerate for at least 2 hours or overnight.

2. Soak wooden skewers in water while the chicken is marinating.

3. Preheat the oven to 450°F.

4. Skewer one piece of chicken per stick, saving any remaining marinade. Place on a foil or parchment-lined baking sheet and bake for about 15 minutes until chicken is cooked through.

5. Pour leftover marinade into a small saucepan. Bring to a boil, then simmer until thickened, about 5 minutes.

6. Use a pastry brush to coat the roasted chicken with the thickened marinade. Immediately sprinkle with sesame seeds and chives to serve.

Traveling in a New Relationship

One thing that we have shared since the moment we met has been a deep love of travel. We love exploring different worlds, savoring new flavors, and going on adventures together. And there's nothing that can make or break a budding relationship like taking an audacious trip together.

Whether it's a romantic weekend getaway or an international adventure, you will learn new things about your partner and get a trial run at cohabiting, albeit in hotel rooms with room service or hostels with bunkmates.

Our first trip together was also one of our most daring: five months after we started dating, we rented a car in South Africa and traversed the country for the World Cup in 2010. One of Ned's buddies (yes, those same buddies) was working for a year in a small town outside Johannesburg during the World Cup. Ned couldn't resist the chance to go, and to his surprise, when he invited Ariel to come with him to crash on a couch for an adventure across the world, she jumped right in.

Traveling to a foreign country together was a bonding experience like no other. First, we had a 72-hour layover in Paris, where Ariel showed Ned all of her favorite arrondissements from when she lived there over her gap year. Then we arrived in South Africa, figured out how to buy a SIM card, and picked up a car (it came with mandatory collision insurance—more on that later). It was our first time driving on the opposite side of the road, and Ned nearly got into an accident pulling out of the rental facility. Our first stop was Kruger National Park, a game reserve where you are allowed to drive your tiny rental car right onto the savannah. We saw baby elephants, baby giraffes, lions, dozens of zebras, even some enormous hippos. It was magical.

In the evening, we had our first *braai,* or barbecue, and Ned tasted *boerewors*, a savory beef sausage full of spices and rich with fatty deliciousness, and *pap*, the best type of traditional porridge. Take a scoop of pap, mix it with your grilled protein of choice, and enjoy as the juices mingle with the satisfying polenta-like texture of the porridge. It was a family affair, and we got to meet many of the other people in the community in which we were staying.

Next, we stopped in a town called Mtubatuba

Ned ready for a soccer game in Brazil

to visit Ned's friend, who was working at a soccer training academy. Ned has always been an adventurous eater and, just like the braai, he went all in on a simmered, smoky, spicy lamb curry. Unfortunately, for whatever reason, the lamb didn't sit right with his poor American belly, and the next day Ariel had to drive all 10 hours from Durban to Port Elizabeth by herself, pulling over every hour so Ned could take care of business.

When we finally arrived in Port Elizabeth, the soccer match caused so much traffic and confusion that we got into a fender bender. It was the final straw. Ariel wanted to go home. Ned was still queasy. A magical trip was turning sour.

But we got through it. Ned recovered and was able to drive to Cape Town, where Ariel rediscovered the joy of exploration along the waterfront and we were both reinvigorated. Although it was stressful at the time, the experience bonded the two of us for life, and we realized that if we could handle the chaos of food poisoning and traffic accidents in a foreign country together, there wasn't much we couldn't handle.

Ariel ready for a crab harvest in Seattle

On the California Coast with a rented Mustang convertible

Sightseeing in China

Chicken and Potato Hand Pies

MAKES 8 HAND PIES

Inspired by a traditional English meat pie lunch that can also be found here in Cali (hello, empanadas!), these are great, hearty fare for those long travel days in the car. Wrap in paper instead of plastic so they don't get too soggy, and you can have a proper picnic wherever you are!

INGREDIENTS

3 tablespoons olive oil

1 pound (about 2) chicken breasts, cut into 1-inch pieces

Salt and pepper, to taste

1 medium yellow onion, diced

½ cup frozen peas, thawed

4 cloves garlic, sliced

2 tablespoons all-purpose flour

2 teaspoons ground cumin

1 teaspoon ground coriander

¼ teaspoon ground ginger

Pinch of ground cinnamon

¾ cup chicken stock

¾ pound (12 ounces) waxy potatoes, cut into ½-inch cubes

¼ cup chopped parsley

1 pie crust, rolled out (store-bought or homemade, page 216)

1 large egg, beaten with a pinch of salt

INSTRUCTIONS

1. Preheat the oven to 375°F.

2. Heat a wide nonstick pan over medium heat. Add 2 tablespoons oil and then the chicken, cooking until browned, 4 to 5 minutes. Season with salt and pepper. Remove chicken from the pan and set aside.

3. To the same pan, add the remaining oil and the onion, cooking until softened, 2 to 3 minutes.

4. Stir in the peas, garlic, flour, cumin, coriander, ginger, cinnamon, and chicken stock. Stir until combined.

5. Add the potatoes and bring to a boil. Reduce to a simmer, cooking until the potatoes are fork-tender, 10 to 12 minutes.

6. Taste the broth, adding more salt and pepper if needed. Turn off the heat and add the cooked chicken and parsley.

7. Using a small bowl around 5 inches in diameter, cut circles out of the pie crust. Reuse any trimmings by rolling into a ball and rolling out with a rolling pin until there is no more remaining dough.

8. Working with one piece of dough at a time, spoon ⅓ cup of the pie filling into the center of a crust round. Carefully fold in half to make a crescent shape. Use a fork to press together the edges to seal. Repeat with remaining pieces of dough.

9. Brush the tops of the pies with the beaten egg. Use a small knife to cut a couple small slits in the top for the pies to ventilate. Bake for 20 to 25 minutes until golden brown.

Crabcake Burgers with Spicy Aioli

SERVES 2

Crab holds a special place in Ariel's heart. She grew up spending summers in Washington State, pulling crab pots out of Puget Sound with her grandfather. While it's not as adventurous as South Africa, it's one of our favorite places to visit and we go there almost every year now that we live on the West Coast. The whole family spends hours together, picking out every single piece of tender meat to make the perfect crabcakes. Ariel's secret? Leftover mashed potatoes from dinner the night before and LOTS of Old Bay.

INGREDIENTS

6 ounces lump crabmeat, canned or fresh

¼ cup plain bread crumbs

1 teaspoon Old Bay seasoning

1 tablespoon mayonnaise

1 teaspoon Worcestershire sauce

½ cup mashed potatoes (leftover or freshly made, see page 157)

2 tablespoons finely chopped dill

1 egg

2 potato buns

1 tablespoon sunflower oil

1 tablespoon unsalted butter

Spicy aioli (store-bought or homemade, see page 215)

4 pieces green leaf lettuce

2 lemon wedges, to serve

INSTRUCTIONS

1. In a medium-sized bowl, combine crabmeat, bread crumbs, Old Bay, mayonnaise, Worcestershire sauce, mashed potatoes, dill, and egg, and mix well to combine.

2. Divide the mixture in half and place each on a square of parchment paper. Shape each patty into circles about 4 inches in diameter, or the same width as your buns. Cover and chill in the refrigerator for 10 minutes.

3. Heat a wide pan over medium heat. Toast the buns cut side down until golden, then remove from the pan.

4. Add the oil and butter, swirling to coat the bottom of the pan.

5. Once the butter is melted, carefully place the crabcakes in the pan, cooking for 3 to 4 minutes on each side, until lightly browned and slightly firm.

6. To assemble, spread the aioli on both halves of the buns. Sandwich a crabcake and a piece of lettuce between each half. Serve with lemon wedges.

Barbecue Blackberry Cobbler

SERVES 8

Let's stay in the Pacific Northwest a little longer, shall we? In the area where Ariel's grandparents live, the blackberry bushes grow wild on the side of the road in September. We would all grab a random kitchen container—a bowl, a bucket, or a Tupperware container with an inevitably missing lid—and climb into the bramble to get the juiciest berries to take home for cobbler. Cobbler is like pie but less work because there's no crust, and it goes great with crab.

INGREDIENTS

BLACKBERRY FILLING

3 pints (18 ounces) blackberries

⅓ cup granulated sugar

¼ cup all-purpose flour

Zest of 1 lemon

2 tablespoons freshly squeezed lemon juice

½ teaspoon cinnamon

Pinch of nutmeg (optional)

½ teaspoon kosher salt

COBBLER TOPPING

1½ cups all-purpose flour

½ cup granulated sugar

2 teaspoons baking powder

½ teaspoon cinnamon

Pinch of nutmeg (optional)

½ teaspoon kosher salt

1 cup whole milk

Whipped cream (store-bought or homemade, see page 216) or ice cream, to serve

INSTRUCTIONS

1. Preheat the oven to 400°F.

TO MAKE THE BLACKBERRY FILLING

2. In a mixing bowl, combine blackberries with sugar, flour, lemon zest, lemon juice, cinnamon, nutmeg (if using), and salt. Set aside.

TO MAKE THE COBBLER

3. In a large bowl, whisk together the flour, sugar, baking powder, cinnamon, nutmeg (if using), and salt. Make a well in the center and add the milk. Whisk together until just combined—a few small lumps are OK.

4. Pour the blackberry mixture into a 9-inch square baking dish. Pour the topping over the berries, without stirring, and bake for 25 to 30 minutes until the top is a golden brown.

5. Serve either hot or at room temperature with whipped cream or ice cream.

What to Bring to a Party

This is a time of meeting a lot of new people. Trust us: if a relationship is going to work out in the long run, you have to like their friends and their friends have to like you. They don't have to love you, but there are a few things you can do to make those first impressions count. One of those things includes showing up to a party with the perfect food and drink for the occasion.

Ned's personal standby in those early days (and still now) is a bottle of alcohol. You can never go wrong with a bottle of (kinda) good red or white. Rosé or a six-pack of craft beer are no-fail options if it's a daytime party. If you're feeling extravagant, get a bottle of nice tequila or gin, but don't just grab the first Smirnoff you see: take the time to pick something with a cool label that will make your gift stand out.

We also love bringing easy bites like dips, salads, pull-aparts, or homemade bars to complement whatever spread they already have going. Bear in mind that this is their party, so keep it small and don't make any extra work for them. The best dishes take nothing on their part—cook it ahead of time, bring your own serving dish, and don't expect to take home a clean dish at the end of the night. Ariel's favorite party trick is to put the food on a cute new serving plate and give the plate as well as the food. It's no fuss and you don't have to harass anyone later to return your Tupperware.

Bringing a crab harvest to a summer BBQ

Proud baker

Strawberry Tahini Blondies

SERVES 8

Right around the time we got tired of bringing boxed brownies to every single gathering of friends, the blondie serendipitously entered our lives. We were also making our own hummus at the time and could only buy tahini, or sesame paste, in huge jars. We liked to experiment with sesame flavors and found that tahini made these blondies slightly less sweet but even more delectably gooey.

INGREDIENTS

- 16 tablespoons (2 sticks) unsalted butter, melted
- 1½ cups packed light brown sugar
- 2 large eggs, room temperature
- 2 cups all-purpose flour
- 1½ teaspoons baking powder
- 1 teaspoon kosher salt
- ½ cup tahini paste
- 2 cups sliced strawberries
- 1 teaspoon sesame seeds (optional)

INSTRUCTIONS

1. Preheat the oven to 350°F. Line a 9-by-13-inch baking dish with parchment paper and lightly greasing it with 1 tablespoon melted butter.

2. In a large bowl, whisk together the sugar, the remaining melted butter at room temperature, and the eggs until fully combined.

3. Sift the flour, baking powder, and salt into the same bowl. Stir together with a wooden spoon, being sure not to overmix. The batter will be very thick.

4. Pour the batter into the prepared pan. If the tahini is not runny, microwave it at 20-second intervals to soften. Use a spoon to dollop the tahini around the batter, then use a toothpick or knife to gently swirl it through the mixture.

5. Arrange the sliced strawberries and sesame seeds on top and bake for 30 minutes or until a toothpick inserted in the center comes out clean.

6. Allow blondies to cool for at least 15 minutes before cutting.

Spicy Red Pepper and Feta Dip

SERVES 8

Everyone should have a go-to dip. It's not a rule, but it should be. One of our friends makes an onion dip, a recipe she will never share. Another makes a white bean hummus. Ours is spicy red pepper and feta that goes well with anything from chips to chicken wings and makes a showing at all our parties.

INGREDIENTS

1 (12-ounce) jar marinated roasted red peppers, drained

8 ounces feta cheese

⅓ cup extra virgin olive oil, plus additional to serve

1½ teaspoons red pepper flakes

1 tablespoon fresh oregano leaves, plus additional to serve

Kosher salt, to taste

INSTRUCTIONS

1. Combine red peppers, 7 ounces of the feta, olive oil, red pepper flakes, and oregano in a food processor. Blend until smooth.

2. Taste and add salt if necessary. Pour into a serving dish and garnish with the remaining crumbled feta, oregano leaves, and a drizzle of olive oil.

Potluck Provençal Pasta Salad

SERVES 8

The best dish to bring to a potluck or a barbecue is one that you don't have to heat and can sit out with no refrigeration—so no egg and no dairy. Enter the pasta salad. Did we mention we love pasta? We love pasta so much, even our salads are pasta. This one is great because it's tangy and a little spicy, and it tastes delicious cold or heated from the sun.

INGREDIENTS

1 pound bowtie pasta

1 small shallot, finely chopped

½ cup red wine vinegar

2 tablespoons Dijon mustard

⅓ cup olive oil

1 (12-ounce) jar marinated arti-chokes, drained and sliced

1 cup sliced green olives

2 cups quartered cherry tomatoes

2 cups roughly chopped fresh basil leaves

Salt and pepper, to taste

INSTRUCTIONS

1. Bring a pot of lightly salted water to a boil and cook pasta according to package directions. Drain and allow to cool. Transfer to a large mixing bowl.

2. To prepare the dressing, in a small bowl combine the shallot and red wine vinegar. Let stand for 10 minutes. Whisk in the Dijon mustard, then slowly incorporate the olive oil while whisking.

3. Add the remaining ingredients to the bowl of pasta, seasoning with salt and pepper and about half the dressing. Refrigerate until ready to serve, adding more dressing as needed just before eating.

Entertaining as a New Couple

One of the first parties that we remember being together for was a Christmas party that Ariel threw with her roommate when we first started dating. We often joke about this evening because, told from two different perspectives, it seems like two very different events.

Ariel: It was my first year living on my own, so I wanted to throw a big holiday party and, of course, invite Ned. I had only known him for a few weeks, but I liked him a lot.

Ned: The invite—a very cute email—said that it was a holiday bottle party. How many bottles were we talking about?

Ariel: I spent all week planning things out. I thought of where we would put the food, where we would have dancing, and what I was going to wear.

Festive punch

Ned: I knew I would be coming straight from work, so I needed to have semiformal wear that could double as both office and party attire. I wore a white button-down and stashed a jacket at my desk.

Ariel: When the party started I remember feeling like I was basically just waiting for Ned to show up. Everything was all ready to go. The first couple hours went by and he didn't show, so I was completely gutted.

Ned: I also had been excited all week for the party but had to go to a coworker's birthday party first. I remember being at that first party, stressed out that we were running late and trying to drag my friend away from his conversations.

Ariel: Everyone was asked to bring one of their favorite bottles, and as people started arriving, we had more bottles than people. It was raucous and I got very drunk.

Ned: We forgot to get a bottle. I wanted to just go straight to Ariel's party so we wouldn't be late, but my friend thought we couldn't show up empty-handed (he was right).

Ariel: While I agree in theory, once he was hours late, he should have shown up empty-handed—we had so much booze anyway (he was not right).

Ned: We purchased our bottles of wine, hopped in a cab, and finally arrived at the party.

Ariel: My roommate opened the door for them, and I saw him across the room and just felt relief.

Ned: Our faces both lit up. I don't think it mattered anymore what bottles I had brought or the fact that I was running late—

Ariel: Very late—but I was overjoyed to see him.

Ned: I enter the party and it is wild. Bottles were flowing. We were in our early 20s. I did notice, however, that even at that age, Ariel's apartment was impeccably decorated and the appetizers were laid out very neatly and cute, all on a table. Way cuter than my place.

Ariel: I have standards.

Ned: The table for alcohol was another story entirely. I could tell that at one point in the night it began as something

cute, but as more and more bottles accumulated, it looked like an overgrown jungle of booze.

Ariel: I remember I came up with an excuse to show you something in my room.

Ned: We were talking about our favorite travel destinations and you pulled it up on Google Maps. The move was smooth, and I appreciated having a quiet moment alone with you.

Ariel: That's when we had our first kiss.

Ned: I loved your poise and confidence. I think that's when

I knew you were going to be a pretty special part of my life.

Ariel: It's like marking my territory.

Ned: Aww. Well despite each of us having to travel home for the holidays the next week, that was a moment where we both knew.

Ariel: Over Christmas break we talked almost every day and got to know each other through long phone conversations into the night.

Ned: And the rest is history!

Dressed up for a holiday party

Food is always welcome

Mozzarella Monkey Bread

SERVES 8

Even if alcohol is the main event of your party (as it clearly was at Ariel's Christmas bottle party), you should always provide food. Chips and pretzels are great, but something homemade can really make guests feel special. We have never met a pull-apart we didn't like. It turns an appetizer into a group activity! And this one comes with a surprise. Instead of plain breadsticks, our version of these pizza-inspired dough balls explode with cheese when you bite into them. Serve with marinara to complete the experience.

INGREDIENTS

Olive oil for pan

4 tablespoons (½ stick) unsalted butter, melted

10 cloves garlic, minced

1 teaspoon dried oregano

1 cup grated Parmesan

16 ounces plain pizza dough (store-bought or homemade, see page 214)

6 ounces low-moisture mozzarella, cut into 24 cubes

Flaky sea salt

Marinara sauce (store-bought or homemade, see page 215)

INSTRUCTIONS

1. Preheat the oven to 450°F. Lightly brush a 12-inch cast-iron pan with olive oil.

2. In a small mixing bowl, combine the butter, garlic, oregano, and Parmesan. Set aside.

3. Divide the pizza dough into 24 pieces. Working one piece at a time, flatten a piece of dough and place a cube of mozzarella in the center. Bring the edges of the dough toward the center to enclose the cheese, forming a ball. Pinch the seams of the dough together and twist to close. Continue with the remaining dough pieces.

4. Arrange the dough balls in the skillet.

5. Spoon your garlic-butter mixture over the top and sprinkle all over with sea salt. Bake until the dough has puffed up and is a golden brown color, about 20 minutes.

6. Serve with marinara sauce.

CHAPTER 3.

Disappointment

You need to talk about something that's been bothering you. Conflicts are bound to come up in any healthy relationship. Maybe you lost your job, or you really don't like when he invites that one friend to drinks. You still have to eat. You may not have time to cook or you may have to diffuse a difficult situation, so these recipes are for those evenings where things may get a little tense.

Bright Arugula Gimlet

Vegan Lemon and Broccoli Bow Ties

Massaged Kale Caesar

El Diablo Tequila Cocktail

Jumbo Shrimp "Ceviche"

Freezer Cookie Dough Bites

Tex-Mex Migas

Savory French Toast

Kitchen Sink Nachos with Refried Black Beans

Ned's Favorite Sear-and-Blast Steak

Ariel's Favorite Lemon Salmon Piccata

Kiss & Make Up Flourless Chocolate Cake

Why Are You Mad?

There is not a single person in a serious relationship who doesn't have moments of doubt or disappointment—and we are no different. Instagram and other social media apps can make relationships look picture-perfect, but it's completely normal to be frustrated in your relationship or to disagree. It doesn't mean that your relationship is destined to fail. On the contrary, having those difficult conversations can make your relationship stronger—it's just a matter of how you approach them.

It's normal to be annoyed if your partner left a pile of dirty laundry in the bathroom or they showed up an hour late to your friend's baby shower because they got caught up in a video game. As a couple, we've found that it is best to deal with these issues head-on. When the time feels right, calmly express the fact that you were disappointed.

If your partner is willing to change their behavior, great. If not, it's up to you to decide if that's a compromise you're willing to make to stay in the relationship.

You might also get wound up sometimes when things just aren't going quite the way you expected or you find yourself thinking your partner isn't who you thought they were. These feelings are a little more difficult to deal with because there isn't a specific problem to deal with; rather, it's a general feeling of disappointment. For example, when she was in her twenties, Ariel had a boyfriend who was routinely rude to servers, but it was never so obvious on a day-to-day basis that she felt like she could bring it up to him. Likewise, Ned had a girlfriend who always took a pessimistic attitude toward situations, and Ned could never really pinpoint why her demeanor always made him feel down. From our experience, it's important to identify the way your partner's actions make you feel—sad, isolated, angry, ashamed, frustrated—and to address those feelings.

The bottom line is: check your expectations. Don't lower your standards on what you find most important; for us, those things are honesty and humor. But do keep an open mind about everything else and try to work through it together. Perfection is not an option, but you can expect effort from your partner. At the end of the day, don't be afraid to walk away if the relationship isn't working or you find yourself compromising on your core beliefs. No matter how long you have been in a relationship, you always have the power to do what is right for you.

Bright Arugula Gimlet

SERVES 2

Lime and spicy arugula are just the solution to help get you through a difficult conversation. For us personally, a little bit of gin never hurts when it's time to deal with our issues head on. Refreshing and offbeat, this drink helps us see things from a different perspective.

INGREDIENTS

1 to 1½ ounces fresh arugula

1 ounce simple syrup (store-bought or homemade, see page 216)

1½ ounces lime juice

3 ounces gin

2 lime slices, to serve

INSTRUCTIONS

1. Combine the arugula and simple syrup in a mixing glass and lightly muddle.

2. Add lime juice and gin to the mixing glass and fill with ice.

3. Top the glass with a shaker tin and shake for 5 to 10 seconds.

4. Pour mixture through a fine strainer to remove arugula.

5. Separate stained mixture evenly into two rocks glasses with ice.

6. Add a slice of lime for garnish.

Fizzy Arugula Limeade (Nonalcoholic)

SERVES 2

INGREDIENTS

2 ounces fresh arugula

2 ounces simple syrup (store-bought or homemade, see page 216)

2 ounces lime juice

12 ounces seltzer

2 lime slices, to serve

INSTRUCTIONS

1. Combine the arugula and simple syrup in a mixing glass and lightly muddle.

2. Add lime juice to the mixing glass and fill with ice.

3. Top the glass with a shaker tin and shake for 5 to 10 seconds.

4. Pour mixture through a fine strainer to remove arugula.

5. Separate stained mixture evenly into two tall glasses with ice.

6. Fill glasses with seltzer.

7. Add a slice of lime for garnish.

Vegan Lemon and Broccoli Bow Ties

SERVES 2, WITH LEFTOVERS

Simple and satisfying. If you know it's time to talk about that bachelor party you wound up spending half your paycheck on and you know it's going to be a tough conversation, take 20 minutes to sit down and share a quick meal. Difficulties look a lot less difficult on a full stomach.

INGREDIENTS

1½ pounds broccoli florets

¼ cup olive oil

Salt and pepper, to taste

½ pound bow tie pasta

¼ cup pine nuts

3 cloves garlic, sliced

1 teaspoon chili flakes

**Juice and zest of 2 lemons
(⅓ cup juice)**

INSTRUCTIONS

1. Preheat the oven to 450°F.

2. On a parchment-lined baking sheet, toss broccoli in 3 tablespoons of olive oil. Season with salt and pepper and roast until slightly charred, 15 to 20 minutes.

3. Bring a pot of lightly salted water to a boil and cook pasta according to package directions. Drain and allow to cool. Reserve ¼ cup of the cooking liquid.

4. In a large frying pan set over medium-low heat, toast the pine nuts until fragrant and lightly brown. Set pine nuts aside, lowering the heat to medium-low.

5. Add the remaining tablespoon of olive oil, the garlic, and chili flakes and cook until fragrant, about 2 minutes. Add in the reserved cooking liquid, lemon juice, and zest and bring to a simmer. Add in the cooked pasta and roasted broccoli and toss until well coated. Remove from the heat and garnish with the toasted pine nuts.

Fighting about Finances

We distinctly remember our first fight. We were young and didn't make much money when we met, so we were trying to save. Ariel had bought a pair of pants and a few new springtime tops for about $100 without telling Ned. At the time, $100 was the entire monthly budget for anything outside of the necessities like rent and food. Ned was shocked. Shouldn't we have talked about this beforehand? Ariel was hurt. Shouldn't she have the ability to make her own financial decisions? The fight stemmed from a lack of communication as well as a difference in perspective, as many often do.

While we are lucky to have both been raised with healthy and realistic attitudes toward money, there were, of course, differences we needed to discuss and sort through. For example, Ariel had owned a credit card since she was a teenager in an effort to build credit and learn to use it, while Ned didn't have his own credit card when they met, in an effort to avoid potentially getting too much credit card debt as a young adult. Ned tracked his budgets on statements and spreadsheets, while Ariel tracked her spending with an app. Each approach was valid, but when they collided they required a conversation to understand each other.

Our solution was that we would make a monthly "shared" budget, in addition to our individual budgets, with a joint checking account where we each would contribute a certain amount of money. Also, we set a threshold for large purchases. Below it, you could spend whatever you wanted; above it, you needed to have a shared conversation (in 2010, we determined the amount was $60). The mutual respect and solution-oriented problem-solving styles that we started to develop with each other were yet another sign that our relationship was something special. Even disagreements can be opportunities to deepen the connection you have with each other!

Massaged Kale Caesar

SERVES 2

Ned has never been a huge fan of salads. To him, a salad is
a sad pile of spinach with some ranch poured on top. But a
salad can actually be very quick, easy, and delicious with a little
prep. Ariel likes to add color to salads by way of cooked elements such as chicken and fresh croutons. We included this
one because Ned thinks that massaging kale is a hilarious and
stress relieving experience.

INGREDIENTS

SALAD
1 (9- to 10-ounce) chicken breast
Olive oil
Salt and pepper, to taste
1 bunch (8 ounces) green kale
Parmesan shavings

CROUTONS
2 tablespoons olive oil
2 tablespoons grated Parmesan
½ teaspoon kosher salt
**4 ounces crusty sourdough loaf
torn into 1-inch pieces (about
3 cups)**

DRESSING
½ cup whole milk yogurt
1 tablespoon lemon juice
⅓ cup grated Parmesan cheese
**½ teaspoon freshly ground black
pepper**
2 tablespoons olive oil
**2 teaspoons Worcestershire
sauce**
1 garlic clove, grated
½ teaspoon kosher salt

INSTRUCTIONS

1. Preheat the oven to 400°F.

2. Place the chicken on a baking sheet lined with parchment paper.
   Drizzle with olive oil and season with salt and pepper. Bake for
   15 minutes or until the internal temperature reaches 165°F. Set
   aside.

3. On a separate baking sheet, prepare croutons by pouring olive oil,
   Parmesan, and salt over torn bread. Bake for 15 minutes or until
   crunchy.

4. To make the dressing, combine all of the ingredients in a blender.
   Blend until smooth.

5. Remove the stem from the kale by using a sharp paring knife to
   cut along each side of the stem. Finely chop leaves and place in a
   large mixing bowl. Add ½ teaspoon of kosher salt and massage for
   about 2 minutes until the kale has softened.

6. Add all the elements together and serve with Parmesan shavings.

El Diablo Tequila Cocktail

SERVES 2

While we don't recommend having a difficult discussion after a night of drinking, sometimes a cocktail can cool us off just enough to hear what the other person is saying. Ned will offer to mix some drinks if we have something difficult to talk about (maybe because he's feeling guilty?). We often find that once the drink is gone it's either time to take a break or move on to something less heated.

INGREDIENTS

1 ounce simple syrup (store-bought or homemade, see page 216)

1½ ounces fresh lime juice

1½ ounces pomegranate juice

3 ounces tequila

6 to 8 ounces ginger beer

2 lime slices, to serve

INSTRUCTIONS

1. Pour the simple syrup, lime juice, pomegranate juice, and tequila into a mixing glass with ice.

2. Top with shaking tin and shake for 5 to 10 seconds.

3. Pour mixture evenly into two tall glasses.

4. Fill glasses with ginger beer.

5. Garnish with a slice of lime.

El Diablo Cocktail (Nonalcoholic)

SERVES 2

INGREDIENTS

2 ounces simple syrup (store-bought or homemade, see page 216)

2 ounces fresh lime juice

2 ounces pomegranate juice

8 ounces ginger beer

2 lime slices, to serve

INSTRUCTIONS

1. Pour the simple syrup, lime juice, and pomegranate juice into a mixing glass with ice.

2. Top with shaking tin and shake for 5 to 10 seconds.

3. Pour mixture evenly into two tall glasses.

4. Fill glasses with ginger beer.

5. Garnish with a slice of lime.

Jumbo Shrimp "Ceviche"

SERVES 2

This is our favorite easy meal when tempers are just too hot to turn on the stove or oven. Normally the citrus in a ceviche works to cook the protein, but chopped and precooked shrimp saves even that trouble. We serve it in one big bowl with tortilla chips so we're forced to share. There's something about watching your partner try to balance "ceviche" on a chip that lightens the tension.

INGREDIENTS

½ pound cooked shrimp (peeled and deveined), cut into ½-inch pieces

Handful cilantro, roughly chopped

½ small red onion, thinly sliced

2 tablespoons freshly squeezed lime juice

1 cup quartered cherry tomatoes

½ jalapeño, finely chopped (optional)

Salt and pepper, to taste

1 Hass avocado, peeled and diced

Tortilla chips, to serve

INSTRUCTIONS

1. Combine all ingredients, apart from the avocado and tortilla chips, in a large bowl. Season with salt and pepper to taste. Refrigerate until ready to serve.

2. Add the diced avocado when ready to serve and serve with tortilla chips.

Never Go to Bed Angry

In addition to bigger things like finances, early on in our relationship we also had our fair share of fights about silly things. In 2010, we were working lots of late nights and got an opportunity to take care of a family friend's house and pets for a few weeks. We got to live in this big, beautiful town house in Chicago's River North neighborhood. The first few days were magical. Young twentysomethings going from our tiny apartments to an older family friend's house felt like a free vacation.

But as the days turned into weeks, we started to miss our own space. They had two cats, and we discovered that Ned was pretty allergic to cats—especially when they slept under our bed. Ariel loved the dog and did all the chores for him, but Ned didn't grow up with dogs and didn't know how to help Ariel with doggy care. Little annoyances like Ariel moving Ned's stuff or someone not putting away the dishes started to build. Over dinner one night, we had a misunderstanding about where to spend the holidays; suddenly, it turned into an entire week of passive-aggressive silence and comments about how selfish it was to take the last yogurt. The aggravation grew until Ned found Ariel one night sobbing in the shower. Our free vacation had turned into a trap. If we couldn't work through these trivial issues, how would our burgeoning relationship survive?

We decided to attempt to resolve our issues before we went to bed, since clearly the tiny things were building up into big problems as we went about our long workdays and busy evenings. We sat up late into the night talking things over, and it turned out that a lot of the issues that had been bothering us were easy to fix and that, just by talking about them out loud, we got a better understanding of the other person's needs. Since then, we've always attempted to resolve any disagreements before we go to bed. It's not exactly groundbreaking, but just knowing that a disagreement will get resolved in a timely way makes busy days that much easier.

It was essential to have this foundation to our relationship because, when we introduced a newborn baby to the picture seven years later, it became that much harder to solve problems. In those early weeks of a newborn, we were so tired, stressed, and burned out that, if a disagreement came up, it was very hard to stick to the adage, "Never go to bed angry." We were often too exhausted to talk about anything, let alone a complex emotional issue. So "Never go to bed angry" became "Never go to bed angry unless you're too tired to have a productive conversation, in which case, make sure you carve out time to talk about it tomorrow, when you're better rested."

We'll workshop it.

And of course, after we have a disagreement, the best part is when it's time to kiss and make up.

Freezer Cookie Dough Bites

MAKES 50 DOUGH BITES

When in doubt, head to the freezer. When we were just starting out in our careers, it seemed like every day was long and hard, and we would often come home exhausted and too tired to cook. Some people solve this problem with meal prepping. We solve it with a big batch of cookie dough that can be eaten straight from the freezer (no eggs!).

INGREDIENTS

- **8 tablespoons (1 stick) unsalted butter, room temperature**
- **½ cup light brown sugar**
- **¼ cup granulated sugar**
- **2 teaspoons vanilla extract**
- **1 cup all-purpose flour**
- **½ teaspoon kosher salt**
- **1 cup (4 ounces) finely chopped dark chocolate**

INSTRUCTIONS

1. In a large mixing bowl, use a wooden spoon to combine the butter, sugars, and vanilla extract.

2. Add in flour and salt, mixing until the dough is smooth and no flour is visible.

3. Fold in the chocolate chips until distributed evenly throughout the dough.

4. Use a spoon to shape into a rough ball shape. Place on a parchment-lined baking sheet or plate.

5. Freeze until firm, then transfer to a Ziploc bag. Store in the freezer for up to 3 months.

Tex-Mex Migas

SERVES 2

What would normally be considered breakfast food is fair game when time is short and tempers are high. Ariel grew up in Houston, so she loves adding tortilla chips to a spicy egg scramble to make this Texas favorite. Serve it plain or in a tortilla as migas tacos with lots of hot sauce.

INGREDIENTS

3 to 4 large eggs

Salt and pepper, to taste

4 cups (3 ounces) tortilla chips, lightly crushed

½ cup pico de gallo, drained

2 scallions, sliced

2 tablespoons unsalted butter

1 cup (3 ounces) shredded Monterey Jack cheese

½ cup crumbled cotija cheese, to serve

Handful cilantro leaves, to serve

1 avocado, peeled and sliced, to serve

INSTRUCTIONS

1. In a medium bowl, beat the eggs, seasoning with salt and pepper, until fully mixed. Stir in the crushed tortilla chips, pico de gallo, and scallions. Set aside.

2. Melt the butter in a nonstick skillet set over medium heat. Once butter is melted and foamy, add in the egg mixture, using a soft spatula to stir. Once eggs are halfway cooked, stir in the Monterey Jack cheese. Cook until the cheese has melted and eggs are no longer runny.

3. Transfer to a serving bowl. Top with cotija cheese, cilantro, and avocado to serve.

Savory French Toast

SERVES 2

Here's another breakfast specialty that proves, when in dire need for a meal, you can make anything into a delicious dinner, including French toast. Skip the syrup and throw in some cheese, herbs, and tomatoes for our version of a French toast croque monsieur. Ned likes to eat his like a sandwich, while Ariel prefers a fork and knife.

INGREDIENTS

1 large tomato, cut into 8 slices

Kosher salt

3 large eggs

⅓ cup whole milk

¼ cup chopped fresh basil leaves

½ teaspoon freshly ground black pepper

½ teaspoon dried oregano

2 tablespoons unsalted butter

4 slices brioche, cut into 1½-inch-thick slices

½ cup shredded Parmesan

INSTRUCTIONS

1. Lightly salt the tomato slices and set aside.

2. Beat together the eggs, milk, basil, pepper, oregano, and a pinch of salt in a medium bowl.

3. Melt 1 tablespoon butter in a nonstick pan over medium-low heat.

4. Working with two pieces at a time, dip bread into egg mixture, letting it soak for about 15 seconds on each side.

5. Cook the bread slices in the now foamy butter for 2 to 3 minutes until the bottom is a golden brown. Flip to cook on the other side, adding the remaining tablespoon of butter. Once golden brown on the other side, remove from the pan and repeat with the remaining bread slices.

6. Sprinkle 2 tablespoons of Parmesan into the pan in two piles, roughly shaped like each bread slice, topping each pile with 2 tomato slices. Place the cooked bread on top of the tomato, using a spatula to press them together. Cook until the cheese has melted and has adhered to the bread slices, 1 to 2 minutes. Repeat with the remaining butter, bread slices, cheese, and tomato.

Kitchen Sink Nachos with Refried Black Beans

SERVES 2

Because pretty much anything tastes good with chips and cheese, nachos are the best "kitchen sink" meal when you just need sustenance. Our trick for turning this college snack into a meal is adding pulled chicken and a side of homemade refried black beans for a healthy protein.

INGREDIENTS

BLACK BEANS

2 tablespoons olive oil

1 small yellow onion, finely diced

3 cloves garlic, minced

1 bay leaf

1 teaspoon ground cumin

1 (15-ounce) can black beans, unsalted in liquid

Kosher salt, to taste

2 tablespoons unsalted butter

NACHOS

4 ounces tortilla chips

1 cooked chicken breast, pulled

1 cup frozen yellow corn, defrosted

6 ounces Monterey Jack cheese

1 ripe avocado, peeled and diced

½ cup sliced black olives

½ cup sour cream

½ cup pickled jalapeños

Handful of fresh cilantro leaves

½ cup crumbled cotija cheese

INSTRUCTIONS

1. Preheat the oven to 400°F.

2. Heat a medium saucepan over medium-high heat. Add oil and onion and cook until slightly softened, 5 to 7 minutes. Add garlic, bay leaf, and cumin and cook for 1 minute. Add beans. Cook over medium-low heat for about 20 minutes until liquid is mostly absorbed. Remove the bay leaf. Mash and adjust salt, then add butter.

3. Spread the chips on a lined baking sheet, then top with beans, shredded chicken, corn, and Monterey Jack cheese. Bake until the cheese is melted, about 5 minutes.

4. Remove the nachos from the oven and top with the remaining toppings.

How to Fight Fair (then Kiss & Make Up)

All couples argue. It's an important part of a healthy relationship to voice your feelings and hear your partner's in return. What really matters is the *way* you argue. Conflicts don't have to be emotionally distressing or difficult. Here are our tips for how to have healthy fights with your partner and use disagreements to strengthen your relationship.

Schedule a Time for Conflict

Ever have the same fight at the same time every day? Maybe you're both hungry or mentally exhausted. Change it up. If you have something specific to talk about, like going over budget or job changes, try scheduling a time to talk to your partner when you can really focus on each other.

Listen

Often when someone is telling us something difficult that we don't want to hear, it's easiest to immediately jump to denial or trying to fix the situation. But what we have realized after hundreds of those conversations is that it's not about fixing the situation—it's about listening to the other person's feelings and validating them by really making an effort to understand their perspective.

Use "I" Statements Instead of "You" Statements

Fights often start with the same two words: "You always . . ." And it immediately puts someone on the defensive and makes any kind of resolution incredibly difficult. Instead, try coming from the perspective of sharing your feelings instead of using blame. So instead of "You always leave your stuff lying around," you can start the conversation with how you feel: "I've been feeling stressed out because our apartment is really messy." This opens up the conversation to a respectful conclusion rather than immediately criticizing your loved one.

Apologize

It took us years of arguments to realize that saying "I'm sorry" does not mean that you have lost. It's an agreement that you see your partner's perspective and an acknowledgment that you have upset them in some way. There is no win or lose, or right or wrong; at the end of the day, remember that you're on the same team. Because when you find someone that you really want to spend time with, what matters is that you are both happy and your relationship is healthy.

Ned's Favorite Sear-and-Blast Steak

SERVES 2

For Ned, this recipe actually started out as a personal scientific experiment to cook the perfect rib eye. Ariel doesn't eat beef, but she did promise that when Ned was eating the best steak of his life, she would take a bite just to experience it with him. Turns out this preparation comes pretty close to the best ever, even though the search for the best steak still goes on to this day.

INGREDIENTS

2 (12-ounce) bone-in rib-eye steaks, room temperature

Salt and pepper

1 tablespoon olive oil

4 garlic cloves, unpeeled

3 sprigs fresh rosemary

~~~~~~~~~

TIP: Invest in a good meat thermometer to make sure your internal steak temperature is perfect.

INSTRUCTIONS

1. Preheat the oven to 450°F.

2. Season your steak generously with salt and pepper.

3. Heat a cast-iron skillet over medium-high heat until the pan is extremely hot and lightly smoking.

4. Brush both sides of the steak with olive oil and gently place them in the pan. (It will be hot enough to sizzle, so be careful.) Sear the steaks 1 to 2 minutes or until the bottom forms a crust.

5. Flip the steak and sear the other side for another 1 to 2 minutes. Add the garlic and rosemary to the oil in the skillet and finish cooking the steaks in the oven until the internal temperature reaches 125°F for medium rare, 5 to 7 minutes.

6. Transfer the steaks to a cutting board and place the warm garlic cloves and rosemary on top. Let the meat rest for 10 minutes to allow the steaks to finish cooking off the heat and distributing the juices.

Ariel's Favorite Lemon Salmon Piccata

SERVES 2

When we lived in Chicago, we would often go to a cute Italian restaurant in Old Town near where Ned took classes at Second City. They had a salmon piccata dish that Ariel would devour, then use their amazing bread to sop up the sauce. (You may have noticed that Ariel loves bread and pasta!) It became our spot for special evenings. Ariel mastered the recipe herself so that even now, when it's time to kiss and make up, it's a special treat that fills us with memories of those easy early months of our relationship.

INGREDIENTS

2 (6-ounce) salmon fillets, skin-less (about 1 inch thick)

Salt and pepper

¼ cup all-purpose flour

3 tablespoons olive oil

½ cup dry white wine

2 tablespoons unsalted butter

4 cloves garlic, sliced

2 to 3 tablespoons capers

½ cup fish or vegetable stock

Juice from ½ large lemon (2 tablespoons)

Small handful flat-leaf parsley, chopped

Rustic white bread, to serve (optional)

INSTRUCTIONS

1. Season the salmon with salt and pepper. Add the flour to a wide shallow bowl and lightly dredge the salmon on all sides.

2. Heat a large skillet over medium heat. Warm the olive oil until it sizzles, then place in the salmon and cook for 2 to 3 minutes on each side until the flour has formed into a crispy crust. Set aside.

3. To the same skillet, add the white wine, being sure to scrape the bottom of the pan to loosen any browned bits.

4. Once the wine has reduced by about half, add in the butter, garlic, and capers, cooking until fragrant, 2 to 3 minutes.

5. Stir in the stock and lemon juice, cooking for 4 to 5 minutes until the sauce has thickened.

6. Add in the parsley and place the salmon back into the pan, spooning the sauce on top of the salmon to coat. Serve with slices of rustic white bread for soaking up the sauce.

Kiss & Make Up Flourless Chocolate Cake

SERVES 2, WITH LEFTOVERS

What could be a more decadent canvas to say *"I'm sorry"* than a gooey, fudgy chocolate cake? It's easy to bake, and the rich texture will help you focus on the good parts of your relationship, details that you share and can celebrate together.

INGREDIENTS

8 tablespoons (1 stick) unsalted butter

4 ounces roughly chopped dark chocolate

1 teaspoon espresso powder

⅔ cup granulated sugar

3 large eggs, room temperature

⅓ cup plus 2 tablespoons dark cocoa powder

½ teaspoon flaky sea salt

Confectioners' sugar, for dusting the top

Raspberries, to serve

INSTRUCTIONS

1. Preheat the oven to 350°F. Grease an 8-inch round cake pan and line with parchment paper.

2. Combine the butter, chocolate, and espresso powder in a microwave-safe mixing bowl. Microwave in 30-second increments until melted. Stir to combine.

3. Whisk in sugar and allow the bowl to cool for about 5 minutes, then whisk in the eggs, one at a time, until the batter is smooth. If the chocolate mixture is still hot, your eggs may cook, so make sure to wait before adding eggs.

4. Sift in the cocoa powder and salt, stirring until just combined, being careful not to overmix.

5. Pour into the prepared cake pan and bake for 15 to 20 minutes until the top is no longer runny.

6. Allow the cake pan to cool on a wire rack.

7. Serve warm or at room temperature after dusting with confectioners' sugar and decorating with raspberries.

CHAPTER 4.

Stability

You are taking the next step! Maybe you're moving in together or getting a dog (or a fish). Or maybe it's finally time to bring your S.O. home to your parents (gasp!) for the holidays. It's a huge step and will make your lives easier in some ways—and way harder in others. Embrace your growth as a couple and show off your skills by spending some quality time cooking together.

Netflix and Chili

Tuna Niçoise Dinner Salad

Milanese Chicken Cutlets

Dad's Banana Bread (Adapted from *The Silver Palate*)

Pecan-Stuffed Pork Loin

Fresh Herb Risotto

Buttery Mashed Potatoes

Mediterranean Whole Red Snapper

Strawberry Mint White Sangria

California Waldorf Salad

Pavlova with Citrus Salad

Cranberry Brie Ring

Moscow Mule Punch

Sage Butter Roast Chicken

Parmesan and Pomegranate Brussels Sprout Salad

Tiramisu Strawberry Trifle

Netflix and Chili

SERVES 2, WITH LEFTOVERS

This is for those lazy Tuesday nights where you just want to cuddle in your sweatpants after work. Netflix and chill with our savory Netflix and Chili. If you're feeling super lazy, you can just throw all these ingredients in a slow cooker and let it rip while you chill, but browning the meat on the stove does make it taste better. As far as streaming is concerned, we love anything that involves fantasy and adventure. A shared love of *Lord of the Rings* was something that bonded us when we were first dating, and we still will devour any new fantasy show: *The Witcher*, *Cursed*, *Game of Thrones*—we love it all.

INGREDIENTS

2 (8-ounce) boneless skinless chicken breasts, cut into 2-inch pieces

Salt and pepper

3 tablespoons olive oil

1 medium yellow onion, diced

1 bell pepper (yellow or red), diced

1 tablespoon chili powder

1 teaspoon garlic powder

1 teaspoon ground cumin

1 can diced tomatoes, regular or fire-roasted

2 tablespoons tomato paste

1 cup chicken broth

One 15-ounce can kidney beans, drained and rinsed

1 cup frozen corn

TOPPINGS

½ cup shredded Cheddar

1 cup fried tortilla strips

1 avocado, sliced

INSTRUCTIONS

1. Season the chicken generously with salt and pepper.

2. Heat a dutch oven or a heavy-bottomed pot over medium heat. Add 2 tablespoons of oil and the chicken, cooking and tossing until browned and fully cooked, 6 to 7 minutes. Set aside on a plate.

3. To the same pot, add the remaining oil. Add the onion and bell pepper, cooking until the onion has softened, 4 to 5 minutes.

4. While the vegetables are browning, shred the chicken with two forks or clean hands, then set aside.

5. To the onion and bell pepper, add the chili powder, garlic powder, and cumin, stirring well. Then add the diced tomatoes, tomato paste, chicken broth, beans, corn, shredded chicken, and any juices back into the pot. Bring chili to a gentle simmer, cooking for 20 minutes to allow the flavors to marry.

6. Serve chili in individual bowls, topped with cheese, tortilla strips, and avocado.

Tuna Niçoise Dinner Salad

SERVES 2, WITH LEFTOVERS

It's embarrassing: Ned had never heard of a tuna niçoise before he met Ariel. It turns out it's one of her favorite meals and reminds her of vacations in France as a teenager. Ariel loves the saltiness of the tuna and the olives. We almost named our first child Oliver because Ariel loves olives so much! This recipe is great to throw together for a weeknight dinner when you're both too busy to cook. Just boil a few veggies and you have a gourmet meal for two.

INGREDIENTS

Dijon dressing (store-bought or homemade, see page 215)

½ cup quartered cherry tomatoes

Kosher salt

2 eggs, room temperature

1 cup halved green beans

¼ pound baby potatoes

One 5-ounce package Little Gem lettuce

1 (5-ounce) can tuna

½ cup pitted Kalamata olives

½ avocado, sliced

INSTRUCTIONS

1. If making your own Dijon dressing, prepare according to the recipe on page 215. Set aside.

2. Season tomatoes with salt and set aside.

3. Bring two medium pots of water to a boil, salting one generously.

4. Prepare an ice bath, filling a large bowl halfway with ice and water.

5. Gently lower the eggs into the boiling unsalted water. Cook for 7 to 12 minutes, depending on how runny you like your eggs. Remove the eggs with a slotted spoon and rest in the ice bath for 5 minutes. Once cool enough to handle, peel and set aside.

6. Add the green beans to the boiling salted water. Once bright green, 1 to 2 minutes, use tongs to remove the green beans and place them into the ice bath to stop the cooking. Remove after 1 minute and set aside.

7. To the salted water, add the potatoes, cooking until tender, 8 to 10 minutes. Drain and set aside.

8. To plate the salad, lightly toss the lettuce with 1 to 2 tablespoons of dressing and arrange on the platter. Lightly toss the tuna in a quarter cup of dressing.

9. Cut the eggs in half, seasoning with salt, and arrange with remaining ingredients on the platter. Serve any extra dressing on the side.

Moving in Together

They say, "When you know, you know," and we certainly knew. Our relationship deepened and grew to the point that, a mere four months in, we were ready to move in with each other. After all, we were bringing our toothbrushes over to each other's apartment nearly every night. We usually would go to Ariel's apartment at that time, since Ned's was in a basement, ahem, *garden unit*, with a twin bed so close to Wrigley Field that you could hear the crowd roar and wake up to the aftermath of revelry in your backyard. But even Ariel's first apartment was small, and adding an impromptu third roommate all the time (a.k.a. Ned) made it that much smaller.

We started touring apartments, dodged a few sketchy Craigslist listings (in Chicago, "rustic windows" is a codename for "freezing cold"), and finally found a cute little one- bedroom apartment down the street from where we were both already living in Lakeview. We remember move-in day distinctly. Even though it was just down the block, we carefully packed up a moving van, made several trips, and celebrated the first night by eating take-out together on our living room floor.

It was a glorious honeymoon phase. Finally, we had our own space and could start building a life together, just the two of us. There was so much to learn about each other—Ariel loves moving furniture around for seemingly no reason and Ned loves shopping for electronics. There were so many new memories to create. One of the best parts was it was now way easier to cook together! We deepened our shared love of food and started eating in way more just because it was fun to cook together.

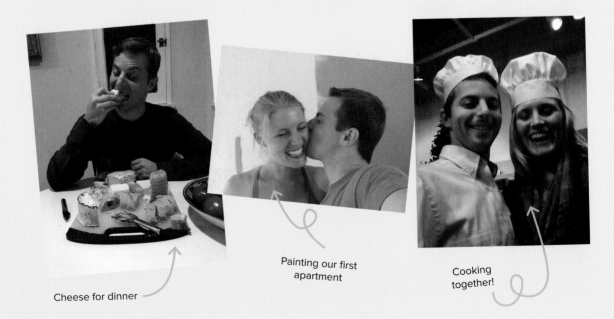

Cheese for dinner

Painting our first apartment

Cooking together!

Tips for Cohabitating

Combine Your Stuff

It's a fact that when you combine two things into one, some things aren't going to fit, so be kind! As a designer, Ariel had a lot of trouble accepting some of Ned's bachelor pad decor, but for it to truly be a space for both of you, concessions must be made. We all like weird stuff that makes us happy, so embrace your partner's weirdness!

Create a Budget

Up until this point, you may have kept your finances separate, but now that you share all those household expenses, it's important to create a budget or determine if you're going to split the bills another way. You will need to consider rent, groceries, eating (and drinking) out, and entertainment. If you're comfortable, opening a joint bank account to pay for select items can be a great way to keep shared expenses in check. Keep your individual accounts, but contribute a set amount to the joint bank account for expenses each month.

Divide Household Chores

Some people say, "If you have to be asked to do a chore, you are already behind." We don't believe this is strictly true. Be forgiving with your partner and open-minded about their habits—have each person play to their strengths. One of you is bound to be more tidy than the other, which is only natural.

Let Your True Colors Shine

We all do funny stuff when we're alone, and once you move in together, there are fewer opportunities for you to be alone and be your silly self. Own it and embrace your partner's quirks with humor. And get a nice-smelling candle for the bathroom.

Schedule Time Apart

Just because you live together doesn't mean you need to be together all the time. You are entitled and encouraged to take time for yourself, so go out with the guys! Trade your nightly sitcoms with bae for a solo bubble bath. Take time to focus on yourself so that you can give more to the relationship when you are together.

Some things are worth compromising for . . .

Getting the keys!

Milanese Chicken Cutlets

SERVES 2

This is my absolute favorite easy family recipe. My mom would make it for birthdays and special occasions, and it was always a treat! As a kid I would get to dip the chicken in the egg and then the bread crumbs, and I remember it being so much fun. You can slice the chicken thin for less mess or pound it out for more of an activity. Ariel and I use it now as a special dish for the two of us when we're feeling cozy. It's great with pasta or just by itself with a little lemon.   —Ned

INGREDIENTS

2 (7- to 8-ounce) chicken breasts
Kosher salt
½ cup all-purpose flour
2 large eggs, beaten
¾ cup Italian bread crumbs
¼ cup finely chopped fresh Italian parsley
Handful fresh basil leaves, chopped
Oil, for frying
Lemon wedges, to serve

INSTRUCTIONS

1. Working with one piece at a time, place a chicken breast between two pieces of plastic wrap. Use a meat mallet or the back of a heavy skillet to pound until it's ½ inch thick. Repeat with the other chicken breast.

2. Season chicken well with salt.

3. Arrange three shallow bowls or plates large enough to hold a chicken breast. To each bowl, add the flour, eggs, and bread crumbs, respectively.

4. Whisk the chopped herbs into the bread crumbs.

5. Working with one piece at a time, coat the chicken in flour, then shake off any excess. Dip into the eggs, then the bread crumbs. Be sure to press the crumbs into the chicken. Allow the breaded chicken to rest on a plate for 10 minutes before frying.

6. Set a frying pan over medium heat, filling ¼ inch high with oil.

7. Fry chicken until golden brown, 3 to 4 minutes each side.

8. Place cooked chicken on a paper towel–lined plate to drain any excess grease. Serve with a lemon wedge.

Dad's Banana Bread (Adapted from *The Silver Palate*)

MAKES 1 BUNDT

You know that one recipe that just screams HOME? That's my dad's banana bread. We have an old *Silver Palate* cookbook that has been used so many times that it has a broken spine and will only open to the recipe for banana bread. At this point, we all know the recipe by heart and have added our own spin on it. Dad has always done all white flour instead of part whole wheat because it tastes more like cake, and I like to add chocolate chips, because, well, chocolate.   —Ariel

INGREDIENTS

- 8 tablespoons (1 stick) unsalted butter, room temperature, plus more for greasing the pan
- ½ cup granulated sugar
- 2 eggs
- 2 cups all-purpose flour
- 1 teaspoon baking soda
- ½ teaspoon kosher salt
- 3 to 4 large ripe bananas, mashed (about 1¼ to 1½ cups)
- 2 teaspoons vanilla extract
- 1 cup coarsely chopped pecans
- ½ cup semisweet chocolate chips

INSTRUCTIONS

1. Preheat the oven to 350°F. Grease a small Bundt pan.

2. In a large bowl, cream the butter and sugar until fluffy.

3. Add eggs one at a time and beat.

4. In a medium bowl, mix the flour, baking soda, and salt.

5. In a small bowl, mash the bananas and add vanilla.

6. Alternately add dry and wet ingredients to butter mixture. Fold in the pecans and chocolate chips.

7. Pour into prepared pan and bake 50 to 60 minutes or until a toothpick inserted in the center comes out clean. Cool in pan for 10 minutes.

Dressed for Success

When you're in love, your relationship can move very quickly. Ours certainly did. What was once a toothbrush that we kept at each other's house turned into a combined moving van full of college hand-me-downs: the flexible yet affordable IKEA POÄNG chair, forgotten posters of Paris, a full set of lacrosse and horseback riding gear "just in case." Our lives were already entwined emotionally, and now we began the process of combining the physical elements, choosing what to highlight or what to give away, and determining who had the better blender (spoiler: it was Ariel).

When we made the decision, we told our parents, and when Ariel's dad heard that his daughter intended to move in with a man he'd never met, he booked the next flight out to Chicago. There was a pretense of business meetings, but the purpose was clear: he needed to meet this young man ASAP.

As the "young man" in question, the pressure was on for me to pull off an impressive yet casual Meet the Parents weekend.

At the time I was temping at a chemistry lab close to O'Hare Airport, which was an hour away, so it was very gently encouraged by Ariel that I pick up her dad, Mark, when his flight landed. The pressure was on. I knew I had to be dressed for success and prove to Ariel's dad that I wasn't just in a dead-end temporary job but someone who was going places. So I scheduled a job interview for the same day that Mark flew in. And then I wore a full suit.

When I pulled up to the airport, we shook hands and Mark said I looked sharp. I was sweating—probably because I was wearing a full suit. He asked if I always dressed like this. I replied no and explained about the job interview. We then proceeded to awkwardly talk about Ariel, our jobs, and our families for the 60-plus-minute drive in traffic to Ariel's old apartment. I explained that I ultimately wanted to work in entertainment but that it was important to me to have a stable day job. He worked as an oil trader; I worked as a research chemist making renewable fuels. We ended up having a lot in common.

For dinner, Ariel mentioned offhandedly that her dad liked pork loin. I had never made it, handled it, or eaten it. I frantically Googled some recipes, found something with a mustard rub, and tried it out. As we sat down to eat, I tried to be casual and charming, internally freaking out that it would all go off the rails somehow. He took a bite. "Not bad," he said. *Close enough!* As dinner went on, our conversation became more and more natural. I started to develop a fondness and respect for Ariel's father that continues to this day. And at the end of the weekend, I found out that I had gotten the new job! Ariel and I moved in together two months later, nesting into our first home as a couple. And whenever Ariel's family comes to visit, I make sure to add pork loin to the menu.

—Ned

Ready to meet Ariel's dad!

Pecan-Stuffed Pork Loin

SERVES 4 TO 6

This is Ariel's dad's favorite dish to cook; in fact, Ned had never even eaten pork loin until he met Ariel's family. Cooking your in-laws' favorite meal is a daunting task, but Ned has mastered the butterfly method. The mustardy, nutty, spiral filling looks elevated and nicely complements the tender meat. Suit and tie not required.

INGREDIENTS

- **2 pieces (2 to 2.5 pounds) pork tenderloin**
- **Salt and pepper, to taste**
- **1 cup chopped pecans**
- **2 tablespoons unsalted butter**
- **1 medium yellow onion, diced**
- **2 medium tart apples, peeled and diced small**
- **1 tablespoon chopped rosemary leaves**
- **1 teaspoon fennel seeds**
- **2 tablespoons Dijon mustard**
- **Olive oil**

INSTRUCTIONS

1. Preheat the oven to 350°F.

2. Place pork on a cutting board lined with plastic wrap.

3. Butterfly the pork loin by cutting halfway into the pork horizontally, being careful not to cut all the way through the flesh. Open the pork so it's shaped like a butterfly. Place on top of a piece of plastic wrap and pound until ½ inch thick. Do the same with the second piece of pork. Season well on both sides with salt and pepper. Set aside as you prepare the filling.

4. Place pecans on a parchment-lined baking sheet and bake for 5 to 7 minutes until slightly toasted and aromatic. Be attentive, as nuts go from brown to burnt in an instant! Transfer to a mixing bowl and set aside.

5. Meanwhile, melt the butter in a sauté pan over medium heat. Add the onion and apples, cooking until softened and reduced in size, 10 to 15 minutes.

6. Stir in rosemary, fennel seeds, and pecans. Remove from heat.

7. Place the pork on a parchment-lined baking sheet, cut sides facing up. Brush with Dijon mustard. Spread half the stuffing down the center of one of the pork loins, then fold over to close. Repeat with the second loin.

8. Tie the pork shut using kitchen twine, spacing each knot 1 to 2 inches apart. Then turn the wrapped loin over so the seam side is facing down. Repeat with the second loin.

9. Drizzle the tops with olive oil and roast until the internal temperature of the pork reaches 145°F, about 15 minutes. For extra color, after the pork has cooked, switch the oven to broil and place meat under the broiler for 2 to 3 minutes.

10. Let the roasted pork rest on a cutting board for 15 minutes, then remove the twine, slice, and serve.

Fresh Herb Risotto

SERVES 4 TO 6

This was Ned's other main family celebration meal growing up. You can take a shortcut on the traditional method of making risotto, but in our opinion the best way to make it is slowly, with saffron. Make an evening out of it and take your time. Ned's mom says restaurants always cut corners and parboil the rice, but if you go slow the steam from the pot will give you good skin. By the way, how do you pronounce risotto? Ned's Italian family always pronounces it ri-sot-tow, and apparently the rest of America, including Ariel, calls it ree-zo-toe. Call it whatever you like: it's the best.

INGREDIENTS

3 to 4 cups chicken stock

A large pinch of saffron threads (18 to 20 threads)

4 tablespoons (½ stick) unsalted butter

2 leeks, trimmed and finely chopped

½ cup diced yellow onion

4 cloves garlic, thinly sliced

1 cup arborio rice

½ cup dry white wine

1 cup grated Parmigiano-Reggiano cheese, plus more to serve

A handful each of fresh Italian parsley, basil, and dill

Salt and pepper, to taste

INSTRUCTIONS

1. Add the chicken stock and saffron to a saucepan, bring to a simmer over medium heat, then reduce heat to low and keep it just barely simmering.

2. On another burner, heat a large cooking pot over medium heat. Add the butter, leeks, onion, and garlic, cooking until leeks are tender, 2 to 3 minutes. Add the rice, coating with the butter mixture and stirring until fragrant, another 1 to 2 minutes.

3. Pour in the white wine and stir, cooking until absorbed.

4. Adding only one ladle at a time (about ½ cup), stir the hot broth into the rice. Keep stirring, cooking the rice until most of the liquid has been absorbed. Repeat with remaining broth until rice is tender. Risotto will become creamier as you go until the grains are al dente. You don't want them mushy! This will take between 20 and 30 minutes. If the rice is a bit clumped together, add another ladle of broth to loosen.

5. Turn off the heat and add the Parmigiano-Reggiano and fresh herbs. Stir. Season with salt and pepper. Serve with additional grated cheese.

Buttery Mashed Potatoes

SERVES 4 TO 6

Ever taken a bite of a dish and known that you would forever try to re-create it? That was us at an anniversary dinner in Monaco after one bite of the mashed potatoes at the Alain Ducasse restaurant. It was the most money we'd ever spent on a meal, yet afterward all we could talk about were the mashed potatoes. We have tried every different way to imitate their silky, buttery texture—from painstakingly mashing them with a fork to whipping them like whipped cream—and we've found that a simple potato masher and some good old elbow grease come pretty close.

INGREDIENTS

2 pounds (about 6 large) baking potatoes, peeled and quartered

4 tablespoons (½ stick) unsalted butter

½ cup heavy cream

Salt and pepper, to taste

INSTRUCTIONS

1. Bring a pot of salted water to a boil, add potatoes, and cook until tender but still slightly firm, about 15 minutes.

2. Drain the water and use a potato masher to mash potatoes thoroughly until no lumps remain. Add the butter and cream and mix thoroughly. Season with salt and pepper.

Tips for Meeting the Parents

We get it! Meeting your partner's family is one of the most nerve-racking interactions you'll have in an early relationship. There is so much stress on both sides. Everybody knows you only get one chance to make a good first impression, and it's been proven that people can make snap judgments in seconds that will last a lifetime. No pressure!

So what if you're not a culinary genius? Or you don't know everything about financial planning? The key to making a good first impression is that you make an effort. Let's see that again in bold: **what matters is you MAKE AN EFFORT.** Parents (and honestly, friends and all other family members) aren't looking for you to be perfect. They just want to know that their loved ones are taken care of and that you care. So care! Care about what you wear when you meet them. Care about making them comfortable by doing your research. You've probably spent enough time Facebook stalking people to have a PhD, so use those skills to find out what they are like, and ask your partner about any weird quirks or things to avoid beforehand.

Also, remember that this interaction goes both ways. While you're worried about what they think of you, they are also in the spotlight here! The whole point of meeting your partner's parents is that you care about your partner and could potentially see them in your life for a while to come. That's a big deal! A parent's influence can be powerful, and you can learn a lot about your partner from meeting their family. Don't judge them any more than you wish to be judged yourself. And no matter what you are doing, time of day, or season, consider bringing a gift and being generous with compliments. Even if it seems dumb or old-fashioned, having flowers or baked goods in hand softens people like butter.

If all else fails, people like to talk about themselves. Prepare some questions beforehand because engaging someone about their interests is a proven tactic to getting people to like you. But don't let the interaction be an interview where you find yourself listing off bullet points on your résumé. Ask questions and engage in a meaningful way. And hey, the more you engage them in questions about themselves, the less likely you will have a chance to say something you regret!

Mediterranean Whole Red Snapper

SERVES 4 TO 6

We love creating low-pressure ways to impress family and friends. Fish is an easy meal that makes a big impact. Ned grew up deep-sea fishing with his grandfather off of Long Island, and now, holidays at his parents' house in Jacksonville, Florida, often involve an adventure out to the high seas for snapper. There's nothing more refreshing than waking up at the crack of dawn, smelling the salty air of the ocean, and (fingers crossed) return-ing with a fresh catch. Fillets are always an option, but try a whole-roasted fish to really impress the family! It's visually stun-ning and surprisingly simple to prepare.

INGREDIENTS

FISH

¼ cup olive oil

4 cloves garlic

¼ cup packed fresh oregano leaves, plus 4 sprigs

2 lemons

1 red snapper, cleaned

PEPPERS AND ONIONS

2 tablespoons olive oil

½ medium red onion, sliced

4 assorted sweet peppers, sliced into rounds

Kosher salt, to taste

INSTRUCTIONS

TO MAKE THE FISH:

1. Preheat the oven to 450°F.

2. In a mini food processor, combine the olive oil, garlic, oregano, and the juice of 1 lemon. Pulse into a rough paste. If you don't have a food processor, use a knife to chop the ingredients.

3. Pat your fish dry with a paper towel, then place it on a baking sheet lined with parchment paper. Cut four vertical slits across the fish on each side.

4. Use a pastry brush or your hands to season the fish with the mar-inade, being sure to coat well on the outside and inside of the fish.

5. Thinly slice half a lemon, then carefully arrange the lemon slices and oregano sprigs inside the slits.

6. Bake for 15 to 20 minutes until the skin is golden and crispy.

TO MAKE THE PEPPERS AND ONIONS:

7. While the fish is cooking, set a medium-sized frying pan over medium-high heat. Add the olive oil, onion, and peppers, cooking until softened and slightly charred, 5 to 7 minutes. Season with salt.

8. Transfer the cooked fish onto a serving plate and garnish with the peppers and onions and additional lemon wedges. To eat it, pull apart each section of the fillet with a fork and then, when you're done with one side, flip it over for the other side.

Strawberry Mint White Sangria

SERVES 4 TO 6

We recall fondly the unique BYOB featured in a favorite Chilean restaurant in Chicago. You brought a bottle of wine, and they would make you a pitcher of sangria for an additional $5. What a deal! In the summer we brought white wine, and we've loved the sweet, refreshing taste of this drink ever since then. This is our version, made with fresh mint. It has a hint of pink to please Ned and white wine (yes!) for Ariel.

INGREDIENTS

One 750-milliliter bottle dry white wine, such as Pinot Grigio, chilled

½ pound fresh strawberries (cleaned and sliced)

½ cucumber, peeled and thinly sliced

Handful fresh mint leaves (around 10)

Lemon-lime soda, to top

INSTRUCTIONS

1. Combine all ingredients except soda in a large punch bowl with ice.

2. Ladle sangria into a wine glass, top with soda, and garnish with strawberries, cucumber slices, and mint.

California Waldorf Salad

SERVES 2

We moved from Chicago to California in 2013, and we must have immediately quadrupled our avocado consumption. There is such an abundance of large, fresh, gorgeous avocados in Cali; we love picking out the "good ones" at the farmers' market on Sundays. We find traditional Waldorf salads to be a little too thick, so this recipe replaces the mayonnaise you might typically find with avocado, oil, and lemon. So simple and sooo California.

INGREDIENTS

1 small ripe avocado

Juice of ½ lemon (1 tablespoon)

2 tablespoons olive oil

Kosher salt, to taste

2 stalks celery, trimmed and sliced

1 cup roughly chopped walnuts

1 cup sliced purple grapes

1 Pink Lady apple, cored and diced

6 leaves separated from a small head of baby lettuce, to serve

INSTRUCTIONS

1. Combine half of the avocado, lemon juice, olive oil, and a pinch of salt in a mini food processor. Blend until smooth. Adjust the salt.

2. Combine celery, walnuts, grapes, and apple in a mixing bowl. Lightly toss in the dressing, adding enough to coat each piece.

3. Serve on top of a few pieces of lettuce, topping with slices of remaining half of the avocado.

Pavlova with Citrus Salad

SERVES 4 TO 6

On the topic of impressing family and friends with your cooking prowess, it wasn't until after we were married that we finally got a stand mixer. It was a rite of passage. Ned accidentally got one that was "industrial sized" and didn't even fit on our counter, but we got way into attempting some of the harder desserts out there just because we could. This pavlova was (and arguably still is) one of our greatest accomplishments to date when it comes to impressing a crowd. It's an effort for sure, but isn't that what you want when you're trying to make an impression?

INGREDIENTS

4 egg whites

1 cup granulated sugar

2 tablespoons fresh lemon juice or apple cider vinegar, to stabilize

3 tangerines

2 navel oranges

1 ruby red grapefruit

1½ cups whipped cream (store-bought or homemade, see page 216)

1 tablespoon honey

A handful of fresh basil or mint, to serve

TIP: The meringue can be made ahead of time and stored for up to 2 days.

INSTRUCTIONS

1. Preheat the oven to 250°F.

2. In a large bowl, use a stand mixer or a hand mixer on high speed to beat eggs until frothy, being careful not to overmix; you don't want it to look grainy. Add the sugar and lemon juice slowly, 1 tablespoon of sugar at a time, and continue to beat until it forms stiff peaks. Test it by pulling the whisk quickly up from the bowl and looking for a pointy, glossy top.

3. Spoon the beaten egg whites onto a parchment-lined baking sheet. Use a spoon or soft spatula to spread into a rough circle 9 inches in diameter. Bake until firm, about 1 hour. Allow to cool to room temperature in the oven with the door open.

4. Prepare the citrus by cutting off the rind and white pith so you can see the citrus flesh. Slice each fruit into ¼-inch-thick rounds.

5. To serve, transfer the cooled pavlova to a platter. Spread the whipped cream on top, leaving a 1-inch border around the edge. Arrange the citrus slices, drizzling with honey and garnishing with fresh basil or mint.

Thanksgiving with Both Parents

One of our most daunting hosting challenges came in November 2010, when we hosted Thanksgiving for our parents. *Both* sets of parents at the same time. This was also the first time they were meeting each other, which made things especially stressful. We felt a lot of pressure to set up the perfect environment for them to meet each other and, most important, *like* each other. Or else we worried that we would be set up for a lifetime of passive-aggressive in-law relationships.

This was also *our* first Thanksgiving together, so we exchanged traditions and made sure that everyone got to do their special thing. Ned likes his stuffing with spicy sausage and Ariel doesn't eat red meat, so we made two different stuffing dishes. Ariel grew up putting marshmallows on her yams, but Ned had never tried that before. Ariel's family always had a pie-making contest from scratch, while Ned was used to making pumpkin pie with premade crusts. Ariel's family traditionally opened a bottle of champagne while they were cooking, while Ned's family might split a bottle of red wine at dinner. Watching the NFL was paramount for Ned and his dad, but Ariel's family preferred Christmas music in the background to nibble and chat throughout the day of cooking.

The biggest difference, though, was in the cooking itself—Ned's mom has a bad back, so she's not up to the heavy lifting of a holiday meal (including a 20-pound turkey), and his dad is a doctor who sometimes had to work right up to dinnertime on Thanksgiving. As a result, Ned's family often would order a turkey made from a local restaurant and only prepare a few side dishes or desserts. Ariel's family, on the other hand, would start cooking at 7 a.m.

The wonderful thing about this Thanksgiving was that we had a chance as a couple to figure it all out. We had a pie-baking contest and watched football while the turkey was in the oven. We had a champagne toast and also red wine at dinner. Ned was in charge of cooking the turkey for the first time ever, so he read a whole bunch of food blogs and then made the big mistake of disagreeing with Ariel's mom over the proper way to tent a turkey. (Hint from Ned: It really doesn't matter and turns out great both ways, so just concede to your mother-in-law!)

By the end of the afternoon, we could truly give thanks because our families were getting along with each other just fine. It was a crazy year for us—we haven't hosted both parents at the same time since—but it was great practice in merging our various traditions and coming up with some new traditions of our own.

Turkey for six

Cranberry Brie Ring

SERVES 4 TO 6

It's controversial, but we love to start playing Christmas music on November 1. We get so excited for the holidays and for hosting family that the entire fall becomes a celebration. To be honest, this dish is quite merry and bright no matter what time of year it is. Ariel's grandmother calls the rolled dough technique "dough gobs" and often makes a version for breakfast with sugar and cinnamon. We turned it into an appetizer, and now our family won't tolerate a holiday meal without it.

INGREDIENTS

1 (8-ounce) wheel of Brie
2 (12-ounce) cans biscuit dough
⅓ cup cranberry jam
Fresh cranberries, to serve
Rosemary sprigs, to serve

INSTRUCTIONS

1. Preheat the oven to 375°F.

2. Place the Brie wheel in the center of a parchment-lined baking sheet with the rind still on.

3. Divide each biscuit dough piece in half. Working with one piece at a time, flatten each dough piece and fill with ½ teaspoon of cranberry jam. Gather the edges to the middle to enclose the jam, shaping into a ball. Place the dough ball seam side down along the edge of the Brie. Repeat with the remaining dough pieces to create two rings of dough balls around the Brie wheel.

4. Bake for 15 minutes or until the biscuits are golden brown.

5. To serve, garnish with fresh cranberries and rosemary sprigs to resemble a holiday wreath.

6. Carefully cut open the top layer of Brie rind to reveal the gooey cheese inside for dipping!

Moscow Mule Punch

SERVES 12

When you're having family and friends over for a holiday, it's a great idea to serve punch or batch cocktails so you aren't stuck playing bartender all day. This version of a Moscow Mule is a crowd-pleaser for Ariel's family and easily expands when friends and neighbors come calling.

INGREDIENTS

6 ounces fresh ginger (about a fist-sized piece), peeled and sliced

One 750-milliliter bottle vodka

6 ounces simple syrup (store-bought or homemade, see page 216)

9 ounces lime juice

3 (12-ounce) bottles ginger beer

4 limes, sliced, to serve

2 cups fresh or frozen cranberries, to serve

INSTRUCTIONS

1. Place the sliced ginger into a quart mason jar or large bowl. Add vodka and let infuse for 4 hours.

2. After 4 hours, strain off the ginger.

3. Add the simple syrup, lime juice, ginger-infused vodka, and ginger beer into a large punch bowl with ice and stir.

4. Add in sliced limes and cranberries for garnish, floating on top.

Mule Punch (Nonalcoholic)

SERVES 12

INGREDIENTS

6 ounces fresh ginger (about a fist-sized piece), peeled and sliced

6 ounces simple syrup (store-bought or homemade, see page 216)

9 ounces lime juice

3 (12-ounce) bottles ginger beer

2 (12-ounce) cans lime seltzer

4 limes, sliced, to serve

2 cups fresh or frozen cranberries, to serve

INSTRUCTIONS

1. Place the sliced ginger into a quart mason jar or large bowl. Add simple syrup and let infuse for 4 hours.

2. After 4 hours, strain off the ginger.

3. Add the ginger-infused simple syrup, lime juice, ginger beer, and seltzer into a large punch bowl with ice and stir.

4. Add in sliced limes and cranberries for garnish, floating on top.

Sage Butter Roast Chicken

SERVES 4 TO 6

This. Is. Our. Favorite. Whole chicken is great for meals with guests or special meals for just the two of us. We stuff sage under the chicken skin and slather it in butter. It's spatchcocked to impress—you can ask your butcher to do this or tune into YouTube to see how it's done—but the technique also makes the chicken tender and the skin crispy no matter who is coming over. The herb rub also works on Thanksgiving turkeys. Please make sure, however, that you coordinate your foil-tenting strategy with your in-laws ahead of time (see page 164).

INGREDIENTS

1 (4- to 5-pound) whole chicken, spine removed

Salt and pepper

4 tablespoons (½ stick) unsalted butter, room temperature

¼ cup chopped sage, plus additional leaves to serve

¼ cup chopped flat-leaf parsley

2 cloves garlic, minced

INSTRUCTIONS

1. Preheat the oven to 400°F.

2. Pat the entire chicken dry with a paper towel. Place dried chicken skin side down on a baking sheet or in a large cast-iron pan and season generously with salt and pepper on all sides.

3. In a small bowl, mix together the butter, herbs, garlic, and a generous pinch of salt.

4. Starting with the opening nearest the chicken breast, stuff the mixture in between the chicken skin and flesh. Spread it into as many spaces as possible, being careful not to tear the skin.

5. Use a toothpick or skewer to poke holes in the skin all over. This will help the skin become crispy.

6. Roast for 40 to 45 minutes until the internal temperature reaches 165°F.

7. Allow the chicken to rest for at least 15 minutes before carving. Garnish with sage leaves.

Parmesan and Pomegranate Brussels Sprout Salad

SERVES 4 TO 6

Nowadays you can get a delicious plate of roasted Brussels sprouts at any popular restaurant or bar, or for take-out or delivery. We've seen truffle-topped sprouts, nutty sprouts, honey sprouts with dates—you name it. When we cook at home, we use a recipe inspired by our neighborhood bar in Chicago, which served them with flaky Parmesan, balsamic vinegar, and the surprising crunch of pomegranate seeds. It makes a perfect holiday side dish or a simple meal in a pinch.

INGREDIENTS

2 pounds Brussels sprouts, quartered lengthwise

2 tablespoons olive oil

Salt and black pepper, to taste

1 to 2 tablespoons balsamic vinegar

⅓ cup Parmesan shavings

¼ cup pomegranate seeds

INSTRUCTIONS

1. Preheat the oven to 400°F. Line a baking sheet with parchment paper.

2. Add Brussels sprouts to the prepared baking sheet. Season with olive oil, salt, and pepper. Roast for 20 minutes until crispy.

3. Drizzle the balsamic vinegar on top of the hot Brussels sprouts, tossing to coat.

4. Transfer to a serving platter, tossing with Parmesan and pomegranate seeds.

Tiramisu Strawberry Trifle

SERVES 4 TO 6, WITH LEFTOVERS

Ariel's favorite dessert in the whole world is tiramisu. Anytime we're at a restaurant, she wants to check the dessert menu just in case they have it. This recipe is a fun mash-up of classic tiramisu ingredients and strawberries and cream. The fruit and cream make it a lighter dessert after a heavy holiday meal. Serve it with a strong after-dinner coffee for the best of all worlds.

INGREDIENTS

32 ounces strawberries, sliced, plus additional to serve

½ cup plus 2 tablespoons granulated sugar

2 cups heavy whipping cream

One 8-ounce container mascarpone

1 teaspoon vanilla extract

1 (7-ounce) box lady fingers

INSTRUCTIONS

1. In a bowl, combine the strawberries and ½ cup sugar, tossing well to coat. Allow to sit for at least 30 minutes.

2. Using a hand mixer, whip cream and 2 tablespoons of sugar in a large bowl until stiff peaks form. Gently fold in the mascarpone and vanilla extract.

3. Assemble the trifle in a medium glass bowl. Start with a single layer of lady fingers. Layer strawberries, adding some of the liquid. Dollop the mascarpone whipped cream, and gently spread into an even layer. Repeat for two more layers.

4. Refrigerate until the lady fingers have softened, at least 4 hours or overnight.

CHAPTER 5.

Commitment

It's official! Maybe you're engaged or have a kid, maybe you made a commitment to not see anyone else—a commitment to each other can be unique to you. Whatever your commitment means, these recipes are designed to keep things interesting and challenging in the kitchen—from new takes on old family recipes to filling out your spice cabinet. Our hope, as ever, is that you are able to expand personally and in your relationship in the same way that your skills expand in the kitchen.

~~~~~~~~~

Nonno's Lamb Ragu

Confetti Tres Leches

Chocolate Soufflé

Chicken What a Catch-iatore

Pineapple Daiquiri

Cauliflower Steaks with Herby Tahini Vinaigrette

Thai Yellow Curry

Thai Basil Chicken Lettuce Wraps

Ned's Famous Homemade Bread

Halloumi Fajitas

Charred Vegetables with Whipped Buttermilk

Spaghetti with Creamy Poblano

~~~~~~~~~

Nonno's Lamb Ragu

MAKES 8 SERVINGS

My grandfather's family—we called him Nonno—came from a small town in northern Italy called Dorno. In Dorno, making pasta sauce was a ritualistic, all-day affair. So many childhood memories of food are from waking up early to the smells of Nonno and Nonna's kitchen. The savory sizzle of the lamb chops and the sweetness of fresh tomatoes was a concentrated flavor I'd never quite tasted before. I remember Nonno showing me his little tricks, like rinsing the paste can to add the extra tomato-infused water to the pot. I learned that cooking has recipes, yes, and precision, but that part of the joy was taking your time and letting your recipes be suggestions rather than rules. In the end, you get a dish that is as satisfying to make as it is to serve to your whole family for Sunday dinner. Just don't add sugar or my mom will disown me. Unless your family is Sicilian, in which case it's allowed and we'll just have to agree to disagree.   —Ned

INGREDIENTS

1½ pounds lamb shoulder, cut into 2-inch chunks

Salt and pepper

3 tablespoons olive oil

1 medium onion, finely chopped

1 (6-ounce) can good tomato paste

2 (24-ounce) cans crushed San Marzano tomatoes

¾ cup water

¼ cup roughly chopped fresh flat-leaf parsley

1 cup fresh basil, plus additional to serve

Pasta, to serve

INSTRUCTIONS

1. Season the lamb generously with salt and black pepper.

2. In a heavy-bottomed pot or Dutch oven set over medium heat, brown the lamb using 2 tablespoons of olive oil. Once all sides of the lamb have browned, remove and set aside.

3. To the same pot, add another tablespoon of oil. Cook the onion until softened, 3 to 5 minutes.

4. Stir in the tomato paste, cooking until it turns to a dark red. Fill the empty paste can with water, about ¾ cup.

5. Add the crushed tomatoes, the water from the paste can, parsley, basil, and browned lamb to the pot and bring to a gentle boil. Once the mixture is bubbly, lower the heat to a very slow simmer.

6. Cover with a lid and stir occasionally throughout cooking to make sure the sauce doesn't stick to the bottom of the pot. Simmer for at least 1½ hours, until the lamb is fork tender and starts to pull apart.

7. Adjust the amount of salt, pepper, and basil to taste. Serve with your choice of pasta, garnishing with basil leaves.

Confetti Tres Leches

MAKES 12 SERVINGS

While it's not a family recipe, tres leches cake reminds me of my dad. He loves to bake and has always been really good at it. Growing up, his baked goods were a treat that we would look forward to on every special occasion—pies on holidays, breads on long weekends, cakes and cookies for birthdays and bake sales—they all made the cut. This tres leches cake was one of his most triumphant successes, and we've updated the recipe here to make it even more fun. He makes it when we're all together in Texas during the summer holidays. It's wet and sweet and best served cold, and it always keeps us coming back for more (no matter how far away we may be).   —Ariel

INGREDIENTS

8 tablespoons (1 stick) unsalted butter, room temperature

2 cups granulated sugar

4 large eggs

2⅔ cups all-purpose flour

1½ teaspoons baking powder

1 teaspoon kosher salt

2¼ cups Fruity Pebbles cereal

2⅓ cups heavy cream

1 can evaporated milk

1 can condensed milk

INSTRUCTIONS

1. Preheat the oven to 350°F. Line a 9-by-13-inch cake pan with parchment paper.

2. In a large mixing bowl, use an electric hand mixer or stand mixer to beat together the butter and sugar until pale and fluffy, 2 to 3 minutes.

3. Beat in the eggs, adding one at a time.

4. Add in the flour, baking powder, and salt, mixing together just until there is very little flour visible.

5. Sprinkle in 2 cups of the Fruity Pebbles, using a soft spatula to gently fold the cereal into the cake batter.

6. Pour the cake batter into the prepared cake pan and bake for 20 to 25 minutes or until a toothpick inserted in the center comes out clean. Allow to cool to room temperature.

7. While the cake is cooling, in a mixing bowl whisk together ⅓ cup heavy cream, evaporated milk, and condensed milk.

8. Use a fork or chopstick to poke holes in the top of the cooled cake. Pour the entire milk mixture on top of the cake. Allow the cake to absorb the milk mixture for at least 30 minutes.

9. When ready to serve. Use a mixer to beat the remaining 2 cups heavy cream until stiff peaks form. Spread the whipped cream into an even layer on top of the cake, then sprinkle the remaining ¼ cup Fruity Pebbles on top.

Chocolate Soufflé

SERVES 2

Soufflé is undoubtedly a test of skill and commitment. We like to attempt making soufflé out of the sheer audacity of the project. Getting it to rise perfectly is part of the challenge that makes it such a fun activity. It feels good to conquer something epic together, even if it's just a tiny dessert. Also, if it collapses, it still tastes amazing—just dump ice cream on top and pat yourself on the back for trying. At this point, it's a marathon, not a sprint.

INGREDIENTS

1 tablespoon unsalted butter, room temperature

⅓ cup plus 1 tablespoon granulated sugar

2 large eggs, separated

1 tablespoon cornstarch

2 teaspoons espresso powder

⅔ cup whole milk

Pinch of kosher salt

6 ounces finely chopped bittersweet chocolate

~~~~~~

TIP: If you don't have ramekins, you can also use straight-sided ceramic coffee mugs.

INSTRUCTIONS

1. Use a pastry brush to butter the inside of two 6-ounce ramekins with 1 tablespoon butter, being sure to fully coat the bottom and sides.

2. Sprinkle in 1 tablespoon sugar into the first ramekin, swirling it around to make sure the inside is coated. Dump out excess sugar in the next ramekin and repeat. Discard any excess sugar. Refrigerate ramekins until ready to use, at least 15 minutes.

3. In a medium mixing bowl, mix together the egg yolks, cornstarch, espresso powder, and ⅓ cup sugar. Set aside.

4. Heat milk with a pinch of salt until it's steaming and gently simmering. Remove from heat and add 2 tablespoons of hot milk to the egg yolk mixture, whisking quickly to combine. Add another 2 tablespoons of hot milk and quickly whisk, then stream in the remaining hot milk mixture while continuing to whisk.

5. Once the milk has been incorporated, pour the mixture back into the saucepan and gently heat over medium-low, continuously whisking until the mixture has thickened. Remove from heat and whisk in the chocolate until combined.

6. Pour mixture into a bowl and cover with plastic wrap, pressing the plastic against the surface of the pastry cream so there is no space. Refrigerate until cool.

7. Preheat the oven to 400°F.

8. Beat the egg whites in a clean bowl until stiff peaks form.

9. Use a soft spatula to gently fold the egg whites into the cream.

10. Divide the mixture into the ramekins, filling to the top. Bake on a lower rack until risen and the top is set, 15 to 20 minutes. Serve immediately.

Our Wedding

On the topic of commitment, our wedding was a magical evening. It seems like ages ago that we had our friends and family gathered for one of the biggest parties of our lives, and in all honesty it *was* a long time ago. Almost long enough to forget just how involved and nerve-racking planning a wedding can be. For us, the planning process was quite the journey. There were so many small details and decisions in the months leading up to the big day, we were completely overwhelmed, especially when it came to the food and drink choices.

Our first decision was whether we should hire a wedding planner or do it all ourselves. We interviewed a very sweet professional who seemed capable, but when we gave her our overall budget—a number so large to us we wondered why we were not eloping—she sharply inhaled and said, "Oh, that's it? With my fee and everything??" It turned out her fee was $12,000. We didn't have that kind of money.

Needless to say, we planned the wedding ourselves.

Ariel got very invested in the process. Spreadsheets with timelines, Pinterest pages for inspiration, catering options. We debated a live band versus a DJ (we both preferred a live band), plated meals versus a buffet (we went with a buffet), and whether to order a photo booth (always get the photo booth!). Once we selected a caterer, we began the delightful process of planning a menu for everyone. And the best part? We got to taste every dish ahead of time! It's a good thing we did because on the actual day of the wedding, we hardly had time to savor our own food.

True to form, we couldn't decide on one thing, so we chose EVERYTHING. The cake had three tiers that were all different types of cake, and the meal had a really fun theme: food stations that tell the story of where we are from. One was Chicago themed, a reference to our home city at the time; one was Italian, to honor Ned's family traditions; and the final one was Tex-Mex, a reference to Ariel's childhood home of Houston, Texas. Come to think of it, the meal was a little bit like this cookbook actually—good food with a story to go with it.

The actual day of our wedding was a blur. Ned woke up for an early morning swim in Lake Michigan with his best man, Eric, then headed to the barbershop for a clean shave and breakfast sandwiches with his groomsmen. Ariel had brunch with her family and friends that was mostly mimosas.

The ceremony was outside, overlooking beautiful Lincoln Park. We were a little worried about rain, but it held off and was a perfect (slightly overcast) summer day. We stared into each other's eyes the whole time and recited our handwritten vows. For a moment the rest of the world melted away and it felt like it was just the two of us. Our first dance was to "Your Song" by Elton John, and the dance for the bridal party that got everyone out on the floor was "We Are Young" by Fun (because at the time, we were, well, young). We danced all night. One of our favorite photos from the night was when we ran out in the middle of the street and snapped a quick photo in front of traffic. There's a garbage truck in front of a red light, and the driver is leaning over and smiling.

Alas, the night eventually had to end. We had planned for a sparkler send-off, but the rain that held off earlier had started to downpour. We grabbed our shoes and hurried for the exit. Almost everyone had a sparkler, and one of our bridesmaids got stuck with the stack of extras that turned into a flaming torch. We ran out, the rain now pouring down on everyone, and piled into our car, flush with the excitement of the most special evening, excited to start our new life together.

First looks

Eating our delicious cake

Married couple smiles

Chicken What a Catch-iatore

SERVES 2, WITH LEFTOVERS

What a catch! You've made a commitment to your loved one and now are riding off into the sunset, taking on life's ups and downs together as a team. One of our favorite dishes from our wedding spread was braised chicken cacciatore, as pictured on page 176. It's the perfect dish for a crowd, but we now like to cook it on nights when we have nothing to do but open a bottle of wine and cook. Feel free to splash a little wine in the pot!

INGREDIENTS

6 chicken thighs, bone in (about 2 pounds)
Salt and pepper
3 tablespoons olive oil
1 medium yellow onion, diced
1 red bell pepper, diced
1 orange bell pepper, diced
8 ounces mushrooms, sliced
4 cloves garlic, sliced
2 sprigs rosemary
1 bay leaf
½ cup dry red wine
1 cup chicken broth
1 (14-ounce) can chopped tomatoes
1 cup green olives, pitted

INSTRUCTIONS

1. Season chicken generously with salt and pepper.

2. Heat a wide saucepan or braising pan over medium-high heat.

3. Add 2 tablespoons of olive oil and sear chicken on all sides until golden brown, 5 to 7 minutes, then set aside on a plate. Chicken may not be cooked all the way through (so no snacking).

4. To the same pan, add another tablespoon of olive oil and the onion, peppers, and mushrooms, cooking until lightly browned and softened.

5. Add in the garlic, rosemary, and bay leaf, cooking until fragrant, then pour in the red wine. Use your cooking spoon to scrape any browned bits from the bottom of the pan.

6. Once the wine has been absorbed, lower the heat to medium and stir in the chicken broth and canned tomatoes. Bring to a simmer and return the chicken to the pan. Add the olives.

7. Partially cover and cook for 10 to 15 minutes or until the chicken is cooked through.

8. Remove the bay leaf and serve from the pan.

Adding Spice

Spice is essential in any dish. It adds flavor and zest, just like passion and enthusiasm can liven up any relationship. The kitchen is the heart of the home, so why not start here when you're looking to spice things up? We love using spices in all of our dishes and are still learning all the ways to combine different flavors. This is a quick cheat sheet that has been useful for us as we've grown our spice cabinet and begun to experiment with different cuisines. This is obviously not an exhaustive list of cuisines by any means, but it's a start!

African (spices vary from region to region): cardamom, cinnamon, cloves, coriander, cumin, fenugreek, ginger, onion, nutmeg, saffron, sage

Chinese: basil, chili, cinnamon, coriander, fennel seeds, five-spice powder, ginger, sesame, star anise, Szechuan peppercorns

Ethiopian: Berbere blend, cardamom, cinnamon, cloves, coriander, dried chillies, fenugreek, ginger, harissa, la kama, ras el hanout, turmeric

Greek: allspice, black and white pepper, cinnamon, cloves, mint, nutmeg, oregano, paprika, parsley, saffron

Indian: anise, cardamom, chili, cinnamon, cloves, coriander, cumin, curry, garam masala, garlic, ginger, mustard powder, turmeric

Italian: basil, bay leaves, chili flakes, garlic, oregano, parsley, rosemary, sage, thyme

Japanese: chili peppers, cilantro, coriander, ginger, karashi (Japanese mustard powder), wasabi powder or paste

Mexican: chili flakes, chili powder, chipotle chili, cilantro, cinnamon, cocoa, coriander, cumin, garlic, habanero chili, onion, serrano and ancho chili powder (among others)

Middle Eastern: allspice, anise, caraway, cardamom, cilantro, cinnamon, cloves, coriander, cumin, garlic, ginger, nutmeg, turmeric, white pepper

Spanish: bay leaves, cayenne pepper, cinnamon, garlic, nutmeg, onion, paprika, saffron

Thai: basil, chili, cilantro, coriander, cumin, curry, galangal, ginger, kaffir lime leaf, lemongrass

A lunch spread in China

Trying Ethiopian food

Pineapple Daiquiri

SERVES 2

We had our honeymoon in Nicaragua a few weeks after we were married. Some of our family did a double take because it was an unconventional destination for a romantic getaway, but we would never take it back for the world. The amazing food and fresh fruits and vegetables were exactly what we wanted on a secluded beach vacation. We spent our days biking into the local town and sipping tropical drinks by the ocean. Daiquiris are an easy way to conjure up the memory of such carefree days, and adding pineapple juice really helps keep that vacation vibe going after you return home.

INGREDIENTS

1 ounce simple syrup (store-bought or homemade, see page 216)

1½ ounces lime juice

1½ ounces pineapple juice

3 ounces white rum

2 slices pineapple, to serve

INSTRUCTIONS

1. Combine simple syrup, lime juice, pineapple juice, and rum into a mixing glass with ice.

2. Cover with shaking tin and shake for 5 to 10 seconds.

3. Pour equal amounts into two rocks glasses.

4. Garnish with a slice of pineapple.

Frozen Pineapple Daiquiri (Nonalcoholic)

SERVES 2

INGREDIENTS

2 ounces simple syrup (store-bought or homemade, see page 216)

2 ounces lime juice

4 ounces pineapple juice

2 slices of pineapple, to serve

INSTRUCTIONS

1. Combine simple syrup, lime juice, and pineapple juice into a blender pitcher with ice.

2. Cover and blend until thoroughly pureed.

3. Pour equal amounts into two rocks glasses.

4. Garnish with a slice of pineapple.

Date Nights

Long-term relationships are comfortable—that's why we love them. But it's easy to slip into a rut if you're not careful. You end up arguing over silly things like dishes or whose turn it is to walk the dog, and you find yourselves doing things out of habit or boredom. We had to work really hard to make sure we still acted romantically around each other even after 10 years of marriage, and date nights are a really big part of that.

For us, Wednesday is Date Night. Early on in our relationship, we had a date night basically every night. But as we were dating for longer, Ned had more evening rehearsals for his improv teams and Ariel was taking night classes in chemistry for an art conservation degree. It became harder to carve out time for each other, where we could solely focus on the other person without distractions. So we settled on Wednesdays as the day midway through the week where we could reconnect. Sharing meals has always been our go-to, especially Thai. Our favorite date-night place in Chicago was this kitschy hole-in-the-wall Thai noodle place called Cozy Noodle. It was a quirky, small restaurant. It had dozens of lucky cat statuettes, license plates from every state, and hundreds of little PEZ dispensers displayed on shelves. And the food? Delicious. There is something so comforting about warm and sweet pad see ew or yellow curry. And since Italian cuisines are our standby meal at home, a cute Thai date night was just outside-the-box enough to feel unique yet comfortable.

When we moved to Los Angeles, we started to explore the Thai Town markets and grew a pantry of curry pastes, rice wine vinegar, and chili sauce. Now Thai cuisine is something that we've added to our home-cooking repertoire, and it's a fond way for us to remember some of our favorite neighborhood restaurants from the past. If Thai cooking is unfamiliar to you, don't worry. It's OK if it doesn't turn out quite like the restaurant (take it from us—it's pretty hard to re-create perfect rice noodles in a wok), but it's a really fun thing to try at home to put some literal spice into your weekly routine.

Chicken snacks on a quick date night

Selfies at a rare concert date

Ned joking around on a night out

Cauliflower Steaks with Herby Tahini Vinaigrette

SERVES 2, WITH LEFTOVERS

It was a huge revelation for us when we realized that not every meal had to have an element of protein. Chalk it up to living in Los Angeles, but these cauliflower "steaks" are just as exciting to make and eat as any meat option. While we don't adhere to a strict Meatless Monday program, we do like to use recipes like this to mix up our routine with more interesting veggie options.

INGREDIENTS

HERBY TAHINI VINAIGRETTE

½ cup tahini

½ cup fresh parsley

½ cup fresh cilantro

1 teaspoon red pepper flakes

⅓ cup olive oil

2 tablespoons red wine vinegar

⅔ cup water

Kosher salt, to taste

CAULIFLOWER STEAKS

1 head white cauliflower, leaves and stem removed

2 tablespoons olive oil

Salt and pepper

INSTRUCTIONS

1. Preheat the oven to 425°F. Line a baking sheet with parchment paper.

2. Combine all the ingredients for the vinaigrette into a blender. Blend until smooth. Add an additional teaspoon of water until the vinaigrette is your desired consistency.

3. With the cauliflower sitting on the cutting board stem side down, slice into 1-inch-thick "steaks."

4. Place on the prepared baking sheet and brush with olive oil on both sides. Season generously with salt and pepper. Roast for 20 minutes until tender and golden brown, flipping midway through cooking.

5. Drizzle the vinaigrette on top and serve immediately.

Thai Yellow Curry

SERVES 2

We took one Thai cooking class in 2015 and never looked back. Our pantry is now stocked with curry pastes, soy sauces, fish sauces, and all the chili oils. Even though our pad see ew attempt was a laughable mushy mess (we'll be leaving that one to the professionals), yellow curry is totally achievable and one of Ariel's favorites. We like to mix up what veggies we put in our curry and found that butternut squash is a great alternative to traditional potatoes.

INGREDIENTS

2 cups cubed butternut squash

2 tablespoons sunflower oil

2 tablespoons yellow curry paste

1 large chicken breast, diced (about 1 pound)

One 13.5-ounce can full-fat coconut milk

2 tablespoons fish sauce

2 tablespoons granulated sugar

1 cup packed, fresh Thai basil leaves

Steamed jasmine rice, to serve

INSTRUCTIONS

1. Place squash in a medium-sized pot and cover with water, bring to a boil, and cook until tender. Drain and set aside.

2. Heat a medium-sized pot over medium heat. Add in the sunflower oil and curry paste, cooking until curry is fragrant.

3. Add in chicken breast and a splash of coconut milk, cooking until the exterior of the chicken is opaque. Then add in the remaining coconut milk, fish sauce, and sugar and bring to a simmer, cooking until chicken is cooked, 5 to 7 minutes.

4. Turn off the heat, adding in the cooked squash and basil leaves.

5. Serve with steamed jasmine rice.

Thai Basil Chicken Lettuce Wraps

SERVES 2

Adding spice is an easy way to make a simple dish exceptional. We eat a lot of chicken and like to find new ways to prepare and serve it. We love these so much we started growing Thai basil in the garden just so we could make them more often. The lettuce is a fresh and crunchy counterpart to spicy chicken, but it's the sauce that really ties it all together. They do pack some heat, though, so be ready.

INGREDIENTS

2 tablespoons sunflower oil

1 pound ground chicken

One 1-inch piece of ginger, finely chopped

1 cup packed Thai basil leaves

½ head baby lettuce leaves, separated

¼ cup chopped peanuts (optional)

SAUCE

¼ cup fish sauce

¼ cup oyster sauce

Juice of 2 limes

3 cloves garlic, minced

1 to 2 thai chilies, finely sliced

3 teaspoons granulated sugar

¼ cup water

INSTRUCTIONS

1. Heat a nonstick frying pan over medium heat. Add oil and chicken and cook for about 5 minutes until there is no raw chicken visible and it begins to brown.

2. Meanwhile, make the sauce. In a medium bowl, combine the fish sauce, oyster sauce, lime juice, garlic, chilies, sugar, and water. Whisk until the sugar is dissolved.

3. Add the ginger and half the sauce to the frying pan. Once the sauce has been absorbed, turn off the heat and stir in the basil leaves.

4. Arrange the lettuce leaves around a platter and scoop a large spoonful of the mixture into each one. Garnish with chopped peanuts, if using, and sauce on the side.

Ned's Famous Homemade Bread

MAKES 1 LOAF

I started making bread after our first son, Wes, was born. I was looking for hobbies that I could do while staying close to home and was captivated by the simplicity and fluidity of bread making. We had just filmed the very first episode of *The Try Guys Bake Bread without a Recipe* and, although my creation was under-salted and dense as a rock, watching the master breadmaker work the dough was captivating. It's a blend of art and science, just like me! Bread making mixes the precision of a scale and flour measurements, like my early days working in a chemistry lab, with the touch and feel of reading a sourdough starter's consistency, just like when I'm on an improv stage or making unscripted YouTube videos. I have a few different loafs that I like to routinely bake, but this sourdough recipe is my favorite. It's inspired by the excellent *Tartine Bread* book that got us through the long days of quarantine in 2020. We add a little bit of spelt to give the bread earthiness and often cheat with a "lazy boy" dash of store-bought yeast because if your sourdough starter is feeling cranky, life's too short to not eat bread. Note: Bread making is typically expressed in percentages by weight, so we have included mass measurements in grams if, like me, you love your trusty kitchen scale.   —Ned

CONTINUED

INGREDIENTS

1½ cups (350 grams) warm water

⅓ cup (100 grams) sourdough starter, half a day into maturation so that it's bubbly and floats on water (store-bought or homemade, see below)

2⅔ cups (400 grams) bread flour

⅓ cup (50 grams) spelt flour

⅓ cup (50 grams) whole wheat flour

2 teaspoons (12 grams) kosher salt

¼ teaspoon active dry yeast (optional)

Rice flour for proofing basket (optional)

INSTRUCTIONS

1. Add 1¼ cups warm water to a medium mixing bowl and add sourdough starter. It should be nice and bubbly and pass the "float test." If your starter is having an off day (not floating, not bubbly) but you still want to eat bread, add ¼ teaspoon of store-bought active dry yeast to ensure a good rise.

2. Add the bread flour, spelt flour, and whole wheat flour to the bowl. Mix together until it forms a tacky ball.

3. Cover and let rest for 30 minutes to an hour.

4. Add the salt and the additional ¼ cup of warm water. Incorporate the salt fully.

5. Now it's time for the bulk fermentation. Watch over it, giving it a turn every 30 minutes by pulling up the bottom of the dough and flipping it over itself. When it doubles in size and passes the "poke test" (usually about 2 hours in a warm environment), it's ready to shape. To do the poke test, poke the dough. If it springs back slowly, it's ready; if it leaves a dent or springs back quickly, it's over- or underproofed.

6. Flip the dough out onto a lightly floured surface and shape the loaf into a ball by flipping it under itself and rotating it 90 degrees a few times with your hands, making a little cupping motion. Try not to use too much flour or work the dough too much at this point. Let it rest for 20 to 30 minutes.

7. Perform final folding of the dough, pulling each edge up and over itself and rolling the dough forward on the last edge so all the folds are on the bottom. You should have a nice little round dough ball. Place it in a lightly floured basket or bowl, cover, and let sit. Rice flour works great if you have it, but all-purpose flour is fine.

8. Watch for a final rise, about 2 to 3 hours, again looking for it to double in size. At this point you can set it in the refrigerator overnight to develop additional flavor, then bake it the next day.

9. After the final rise is complete, place a cast-iron pot or Dutch oven in the oven and preheat the oven to 500°F and place a cast iron pot in the oven.

10. Once the oven is preheated, remove the pot and place your loaf it, seam side down. Score the top of your loaf however you'd like. Common designs are a box cut, diagonal hatches or, of course, an "N" for "Ned's Bread."

11. Cover your pot and bake at 450°F for 25 minutes with the lid on. This will help trap the steam.

12. Remove the lid and bake for an additional 20 minutes.

13. You're supposed to let it cool on a rack for an hour. But we almost always eat it when it's still warm and serve it with salted butter!

Sourdough Starter

KEEP FEEDING IT EVERY DAY AND YOU CAN HAVE INFINITE BREAD!

My sourdough starter is named Sven. He's a little party animal that lives in our house—he used to live on a nice shelf, but then he got too stinky and moved inside a drawer. Sometimes when I forget to feed him he gets a hangover. Once we went to Australia and Singapore for a month and he died. But then he birthed a son; his name is also Sven. The point is that it takes work to tend to a sourdough starter—it's a living, breathing culture of bacteria and fungus. Name it, care for it, and have fun with it, like a little pet. You'll start to notice how it rises and falls, how it behaves differently on hot days versus cold days.   —Ned

INGREDIENTS

⅔ **cup (100 grams) blend of 50/50 whole wheat and bread flour, plus more for feeding**

7 tablespoons (100 grams) warm water, plus more for feeding

TIP: You can experiment with different elements to help kickstart your starter. I have seen others use a dollop of yogurt or a pinch of yeast on Day 1. If you're going on a trip or not going to be able to feed it for a while, put your starter in the refrigerator to slow down the fermentation process. Always use clean equipment. If you see anything in your starter that looks like mold, or that you are not sure is okay to eat, throw it out and start again (or you can always go out and by sourdough starter!).

INSTRUCTIONS

1. Mix flour and water in a small, see-through cup, preferably one with thick sides to maintain temperature.

2. Cover and let it sit out on the counter for 4 to 5 days until it's very smelly and a little moldy.

3. Discard 80 percent of the starter and "feed" it with another ½ cup (60 grams) of warm water and ½ cup (60 grams) of your 50/50 blend. As you feed it, it doesn't have to be exact, but the goal is roughly a 1:1 ratio of water and flour.

4. Give your starter a fun name. It's a living culture, and personification will help you remember. Mine is named Sven and his personality is bubbly.

5. Repeat Step 3 every morning until the starter is predictably rising in the evenings and falling in the mornings, at least 7 to 10 days.

6. The night before you want to bake bread, feed the starter again and then use the bubbly, floating starter in your bread mixture the next morning (about 12 hours after feeding).

Halloumi Fajitas

SERVES 2, WITH LEFTOVERS

Ariel grew up eating Tex-Mex, so fajitas are a staple in our household. As time goes on, we think it's important to continue to try new things together. New flavors, new ingredients, new twists on old favorites. One discovery has been swapping our classic chicken fajitas for Halloumi. It gives it a refreshing rich-ness and sweetness that balances the fresh veggies. Ned likes them with hot sauce and Ariel likes them with medium salsa, but we've written it as a mild recipe so you can pick your own heat level.

INGREDIENTS

Two 8-ounce packages Halloumi, cut into 1-inch-thick strips

3 tablespoons olive oil

1 teaspoon dried oregano

1 medium yellow onion, sliced

1 medium zucchini, cut into ½-inch-thick sticks

½ pound sweet peppers

1 teaspoon chipotle chili powder

1 teaspoon ground cumin

Kosher salt, to taste

1 pack flour tortillas, warmed, to serve

Small handful of cilantro leaves, to serve

2 avocados, sliced, to serve

Juice of 1 lime, plus additional wedges, to serve

INSTRUCTIONS

1. Arrange Halloumi slices in a single layer on a paper towel–lined plate, then cover with another paper towel and pat to remove any excess moisture.

2. In a medium bowl, combine the dried Halloumi slices with 1 table-spoon of olive oil and the oregano, tossing to coat well. Set aside.

3. Heat a large skillet over medium-high heat. Once the pan is hot, add the remaining 2 tablespoons of olive oil, onion, zucchini, and peppers to the pan, stirring occasionally, cooking until vegetables are slightly charred on the outside and a bit softened.

4. Once vegetables are nearly cooked, season with the chipotle pow-der, cumin, and salt. Stir to coat well, then transfer to a serving platter.

5. Lower the heat to medium. Arrange the Halloumi in the pan and cook until golden brown, 2 to 3 minutes on each side.

6. To serve, place the grilled Halloumi slices on top of the grilled peppers and onions. Serve with warmed tortillas, cilantro, avo-cado, and lime.

Charred Vegetables with Whipped Buttermilk

SERVES 2

We like to spend our weekends outside of the Fulmer household, and that often includes firing up the grill on weekend afternoons. We're always looking for new things to grill and found inspiration once we converted a small area of our backyard into a garden plot, which becomes overrun with vegetables a few times a year. The luscious whipped dip is inspired by the homemade buttermilk ranch that Ariel's grandmother used to make, but it is elevated with a little fluff from whipped cream.

INGREDIENTS

WHIPPED BUTTERMILK

¾ cup buttermilk

¾ cup heavy whipping cream

1 teaspoon granulated garlic

1 teaspoon onion powder

½ teaspoon paprika

Salt and pepper, to taste

½ cup chopped chives

ASSORTED VEGETABLES
(SELECT AT LEAST 3)

3 zucchini, halved lengthwise

1 medium eggplant, quartered
    lengthwise

3 yellow squash, halved
    lengthwise

1 bundle asparagus, bottoms
    trimmed

1 bundle broccolini

2 red bell peppers, seeded and
    quartered lengthwise

⅓ cup olive oil

Kosher salt, to taste

Freshly ground black pepper,
    to taste

INSTRUCTIONS

1. Combine the buttermilk, heavy whipping cream, granulated garlic, onion powder, paprika, salt, and pepper in a large bowl. Whip using a hand mixer set to medium speed until stiff peaks form. Stir in the chives and refrigerate until ready to serve.

2. Brush the veggies with some of the olive oil and set aside.

3. Heat a cast-iron pan or grill over high heat. Working in batches, cook the veggies until slightly charred, 2 to 3 minutes each side. Transfer to a plate and season with salt and pepper.

4. Arrange the grilled vegetables onto a serving platter and generously drizzle with the remaining olive oil. Serve with whipped buttermilk.

Spaghetti with Creamy Poblano

SERVES 2

We've come a long way from Ned's poorly lit garden apartment in Chicago. While we still throw chicken on a cold tortilla every once in a while, we joke that the recipe below is an elevated version of the corn salsa dish that Ned cooked for Ariel when we first met. There isn't an easy way to describe how our cooking has grown over the last 10 years of working in the kitchen together, but this recipe, with its mash-up of Tex-Mex flavors and Italian spaghetti, comes pretty close.

INGREDIENTS

- **3 medium poblano peppers, cut in half lengthwise**
- **¾ cup crème fraîche**
- **Juice of 1 lime (2 tablespoons)**
- **8 ounces dry spaghetti**
- **1 tablespoon olive oil**
- **3 cloves garlic, sliced**
- **1 cup frozen corn kernels**
- **½ cup cotija cheese, plus more to serve**
- **Salt and pepper, to taste**
- **Small handful of cilantro, to serve**
- **½ teaspoon paprika, to serve**

INSTRUCTIONS

1. Turn on your oven's broiler, setting a rack on the upper third of the oven. Place the poblano peppers on a foil-lined baking sheet, cut side down. Broil until the skin is blistered and blackened, 4 to 5 minutes.

2. Place the charred peppers in a bowl and cover tightly with plastic wrap. Allow to steam for 10 minutes or until skins soften.

3. While peppers are steaming, bring a pot of salted water to a boil.

4. Unwrap the steamed peppers. Carefully peel off the exterior skin and remove the stem and seeds, discarding.

5. Place skinned peppers in a blender with ½ cup crème fraîche, lime juice, and a pinch of salt. Blend until smooth.

6. Once the pot of water comes to a boil, cook pasta according to package directions. Drain and allow to cool. Reserve ⅓ cup of the cooking liquid.

7. Heat a nonstick skillet over medium heat, adding the olive oil, garlic, and corn. Once the garlic is fragrant, add in the chopped poblano peppers, cheese, and ¼ cup crème fraîche. Stir to combine and bring to a simmer.

8. Add in the strained pasta, tossing to coat in the sauce. Add in splashes of the cooking water to loosen. Adjust the salt and pepper.

9. Serve with a generous sprinkling of Cotija cheese on top, garnishing with cilantro leaves and a dusting of paprika.

Afterword

Love in the kitchen takes many forms, and if there's one thing we hope you take away from this book, it's to make a commitment to cooking and eating with the people you love. Whether it's with our recipes or experimenting with your own, there's no better way to fall deeper in love than through the experiences we share and the food we eat.

We aren't diet gurus or celebrity chefs, but we do love good food and believe that the kitchen should be a place to connect and make happy memories. In this book, you've heard the stories around the meals that are special to us, but, as in life, part of cooking is experimentation and a willingness to go off-script! Let the recipes in this book inspire you and be a guide to mix things up. (We won't be upset—we may even retweet you.)

Some family recipes are not so much time-honored classics as . . . opportunities for improvement. Let this be a challenge to make them your own! Ariel's dad used to avoid all Brussels sprouts because of the way his mom used to make them in the '70s (boiled, with fish sticks!), but he changed his mind after tasting our recipe. Maybe for you it's switching out that can of cream of mushroom soup for some fresh sautéed mushrooms. Or taking that retro Jell-O recipe that your great-aunt loves and trying a fruity Jell-O pie. The possibilities are endless when it comes to cooking, whether you make them just the way your grandma used to or not.

We have come a long way from those days in Ned's dimly lit garden apartment. Between growing our own produce and making our own sauces and bread, the kitchen has become the most important place in our home. It's a place for us to connect over new and shared experiences as well as traditions that date back generations. And while this isn't a cookbook about kids, we have a couple of kiddos now, and it has refocused our mindfulness on what we consume. We decided to make our own baby food from fresh veggies, which is no small feat, let us tell you. When faced with the pressure of giving an infant their first meals of solid (well, semisolid) food, you really think about where that food came from! Ariel's mom used to jar apricots by hand while growing up on a farm, so maybe it's our way of reinventing that tradition.

From those early days dating in Chicago to getting married to moving to Los Angeles, our recipe list has evolved and our palates have changed. But one thing that hasn't changed is that feeling of connection. When we share a meal together, no matter what else is going on in our lives, we retreat to that familiar place of connecting with each other. The whole rest of the world fades away. And for that one moment, you and your loved one are the only people in the world, taking the first bite of a new adventure together.

Appendix: From–Scratch Basics

In cooking, as in dating, time can pass very quickly. If you find yourself needing to move fast, feel free to use store-bought versions of favorite items and sauces. For those who want to take things a little slower, we have included recipes for homemade versions of our most-often used items.

Homemade Spicy Pickles	Pizza Dough	Dijon Dressing
Teriyaki Sauce	Marinara Sauce	Pie Crust
Basil Pesto	Fig Jam	Whipped Cream
	Spicy Aioli	Simple Syrup

Homemade Spicy Pickles

MAKES 12 SERVINGS

Ever tried pickling? We hadn't either until a few years ago, but as it turns out, it's one of the easiest and most delicious ways to spice up any meal. We always seem to have a jar of something brining in the back of our fridge. Our current favorites are pickled red onion and carrot on sandwiches.

INGREDIENTS

PICKLING BRINE

3 cups water
3 cups white vinegar
3 tablespoons granulated sugar
2 teaspoons red pepper flakes
2½ teaspoons kosher salt

CUCUMBER

½ pound thick-skinned cucumber, sliced ¼ inch thick
1 teaspoon caraway seeds

RED ONION

1 red onion, sliced
2 bay leaves

CARROTS

½ pound carrots, peeled and cut into ½-inch-thick sticks
1 teaspoon yellow mustard steeds

GREEN BEANS

½ pound green beans, trimmed
2 cloves garlic, sliced

INSTRUCTIONS

1. Prepare the pickling brine by combining the water, white vinegar, sugar, red pepper flakes, and salt into a saucepan. Heat until it's at a gentle simmer and the sugar and salt have dissolved. Remove from heat and allow to cool to room temperature.

2. Have a mason jar and lid prepared for each pickling item.

3. Fill each jar with your desired pickling item, packing the jars tight. Then cover with the brine, leaving ½ inch of space at the top. Tighten the lid.

4. Refrigerate until ready to serve, at least overnight. Use within 2 months.

Teriyaki Sauce

MAKES 1 CUP

INGREDIENTS

½ cup hoisin sauce
¼ cup honey
¼ cup soy sauce
4 cloves garlic, minced
1-inch piece of ginger, grated
1 tablespoon sesame oil

INSTRUCTIONS

Add all ingredients to a small bowl and stir until combined.

Basil Pesto

MAKES 1 CUP

INGREDIENTS

⅓ cup pine nuts
½ cup packed fresh basil leaves
1 clove garlic, peeled
⅓ cup grated Parmesan
⅓ cup olive oil

INSTRUCTIONS

Combine all ingredients into a food processor or blender and blend into a rough paste.

Pizza Dough

MAKES 1 PIZZA ROUND

INGREDIENTS

1 cup warm water
2 teaspoons active dry yeast
1 tablespoon olive oil
2 cups all-purpose flour
1 teaspoon kosher salt

INSTRUCTIONS

1. Put water in a large mixing bowl. Add yeast and stir to combine. Let it sit for 5 minutes until it becomes frothy.

2. Add the olive oil, flour, and salt and mix until a ball begins to form. The ball will be sticky.

3. Let rise for 30 minutes to 1 hour, until it has approximately doubled in size.

4. Preheat the oven to 450°F. Lightly oil a baking sheet and set aside. Punch the dough down and transfer to a floured surface to knead into a smooth dough.

5. Roll dough into desired shape and transfer to the prepared baking sheet to cook.

6. After the pizza is assembled with your desired toppings, the pizza will cook for 15 to 20 minutes.

Marinara Sauce

MAKES 2 CUPS

INGREDIENTS

1 (28-ounce) can whole peeled tomatoes
1 medium yellow onion, peeled and halved
2 cloves garlic, crushed
2 tablespoons olive oil
1 teaspoon dried oregano
Kosher salt, to taste

INSTRUCTIONS

1. Combine all ingredients in a medium saucepan and bring to a simmer over medium-high heat.

2. Reduce heat to low and continue to simmer for 30 minutes, stirring occasionally and using a spoon to crush tomatoes while cooking.

3. Remove from heat and discard the onion halves.

4. Crush any remaining tomatoes and add salt to taste. Sauce will keep refrigerated for up to 4 days.

Dijon Dressing

MAKES ½ CUP

INGREDIENTS

1 small shallot, finely diced
¼ cup red wine vinegar
2 tablespoons Dijon mustard
¼ cup extra virgin olive oil
2 tablespoons chopped fresh tarragon

INSTRUCTIONS

1. Combine all ingredients in a small bowl and stir to combine.

Spicy Aioli

MAKES ¼ CUP

INGREDIENTS

¼ cup mayonnaise
1 teaspoon hot sauce (we like Tabasco)
1 clove garlic, crushed into a paste

INSTRUCTIONS

1. Combine all ingredients together in a small bowl and stir until combined.

Fig Jam

MAKES 1½ CUPS

INGREDIENTS

1 pound fresh black figs
¾ cup granulated sugar
¼ cup water
Juice of half a small lemon (about 2 teaspoons)

INSTRUCTIONS

1. Pull the stems off the figs and puree the figs in a food processor or blender until nearly smooth.

2. Transfer figs to a medium pot and add remaining ingredients. Bring to a boil, then reduce heat to medium.

3. Stir constantly until mixture becomes a jam-like consistency, about 10 minutes.

4. Store in a lidded jar in the refrigerator for up to 10 days.

Pie Crust

MAKES 2 PIE DISKS

INGREDIENTS

2½ cups all-purpose flour

1 teaspoon kosher salt

1 teaspoon granulated sugar

16 tablespoons (2 sticks) unsalted butter, cold, cut into cubes

6 tablespoons ice water

INSTRUCTIONS

1. In a large bowl, combine flour, salt, and sugar. Add butter and cut in until mixture resembles coarse crumbs.

2. Stir in water 1 tablespoon at a time until mixture forms a ball. Roll dough ball in plastic wrap and refrigerate at least 4 hours and up to overnight.

Whipped Cream

MAKES 1 CUP

INGREDIENTS

1 cup heavy whipping cream

2 tablespoons confectioners' sugar

½ teaspoon vanilla extract

INSTRUCTIONS

1. Using a hand mixer or a stand mixer with a whisk attachment, combine all ingredients in a cold, clean bowl.

2. Whip on medium-high speed until soft peaks form, 3 to 4 minutes.

3. Use immediately or chill in the refrigerator for up to 24 hours.

Simple Syrup

MAKES ½ CUP

INGREDIENTS

½ cup granulated sugar

½ cup water

INSTRUCTIONS

1. Combine the sugar and water in a small saucepan over medium heat and stir until sugar is dissolved.

2. Remove from heat and store for up to a month in the refrigerator.

Acknowledgments

This book was a work of love and it would have stayed firmly in our dreams without the help of so many people. We would like to thank our recipe writer, Kiano Moju, for bringing our ideas and napkin scribbles to life. Our literary agent, Jessica Felleman, who held our hand throughout the entire process—we cannot imagine any better person to guide us through the cookbook world with such confidence and humor.

We are grateful to our editor, Ann Treistman, and art director, Allison Chi, for believing in us and pushing the project to be the best it could be. The entire team at The Countryman Press has been there for us from the beginning: Devon Zahn, Jessica Murphy, Jessica Gilo, Nicholas Teodoro, Isabel McCarthy, and our great copy editor, Natalie Eilbert. Thanks also to our book team who supported us along the way: Sara DeNobrega, Natalie Todoroff, and Deirdre Smerillo.

All the credit for the incredible images in the book go to our amazing photo team: photographer Ivan Solis, food stylist Danielle Campbell, and culinary assistant Jessica Feng, who made it look easy during a time when cooking together was a pretty difficult endeavor.

Thank you to the Try Guys: Keith, Zach, and Eugene, and to the entire team at 2nd Try for helping us make adorable cooking content and putting up with Ned's chaotic kitchen antics. Michelle, our nanny, who helps nourish our kids' bodies and souls while we are writing and testing, and Phil, our lawyer, who is always working behind the scenes.

Lastly, we cannot give enough thanks to our families for inspiring our recipes and being right there with us for every forkful. To our parents, Kathy and Mark and Susan and Jim, and our wonderful sisters, Grace and Danielle. To our brother-in-law, Evan, who not only wrote and tested the drink recipes but stepped in as chef, food stylist, and excellent hand model during our pandemic photo shoots. And thank you to our two beautiful boys, Wes and Finn, who continue to inspire us to create love in the kitchen.

Recipes by Type

Index

Page numbers in *italics* refer to photographs.